TAPESTRY WEAVING

For Peggy,
who was a wonderful friend,
a great support,
and an honest critic.

TAPESTRY
WEAVING

KIRSTEN GLASBROOK

SEARCH PRESS

This edition first published in 2015

Search Press Limited
Wellwood, North Farm Road,
Tunbridge Wells, Kent TN2 3DR

ISBN 978 1 78221 204 1

Suppliers
If you have difficulty in obtaining any of the materials and equipment
mentioned in this book, then please visit the Search Press website for
details of suppliers: www.searchpress.com

Publisher's note
All the step-by-step photographs in this book feature the
author, Kirsten Glasbrook, demonstrating tapestry weaving.
No models have been used.

Page 1

All shall be well
This is a detail from the complete tapestry shown on page 81.

Page 3

Celebration
Size: 16.5 x 23cm (6½ x 9in)
This small tapestry is a celebration of music, dance and theatre.
It was woven from the side (see page 54) using fine yarns, spun
from a mixture of cotton and linen, for both the warp and weft.
The finished tapestry was sewn on to a linen background then
framed.

Page 5

Mask and hands
Size: 12.5 x 23cm (5 x 9in)
This small test piece shows how vertical slits can be left open
to accentuate the fingers of each hand. The cheeks of the mask
have areas of pick and pick (see page 26) which are worked with
subtle shades of colour.

Printed in Malaysia

CONTENTS

INTRODUCTION 6

MATERIALS 8

Warp 8
Weft 8
Frame or loom? 10
Other weaving equipment 12
Mounting and framing equipment 13

BASIC TECHNIQUES 15

Winding warps 16
Preparing weft yarns 18
Weaving the hem 20
Knotting a soumak 22
Horizontal stripes and spots 24
Pick and pick 26
Hatching 27
Diagonal shapes and curves 28
Vertical slits 30
Shading 31
Distorted weft 32
Outlining shapes 34
Cutting the tapestry from the frame 36
Other ways of finishing warp ends 38
Sun sampler 40
Peruvian birds 42
Cat and fishes 44
Simple landscape 46
Cover design 48

FURTHER TECHNIQUES 50

Warp and weft variations 50
Weaving from the side 54
Curved and irregular edges 58
Cushions 62

MOUNTING & FRAMING 66

GALLERY 70

Secrets 70
Give me space 72
The soul needs more space than the body 74
At the still point 76
Journey 78
All shall be well 80
Moroccan courtyard 84
No limits 85
Sacred lake 86
Anna's window 88
Solitude 89
Remember Marrakech 90
Fragments of a friendship 92
One for every occasion 93
Free as a bird 94
Body language 95
Bugatti 96

INDEX 96

INTRODUCTION

Opposite
At the still point
*This large tapestry was woven
on my loom (see page 76).*

Tapestry weaving is one of the oldest forms of woven textile and the basic techniques have remained the same for centuries. The Coptic weavers of Egypt were among the earliest weavers and remnants of their tapestries have been dated as far back as 3000BC. Pictures of looms, similar to the ones we use today, have also been found in ancient Egyptian paintings and on pot decorations. Tapestry weaving was commonly used in small panels on hand-woven tunics, using a special weaving technique, which resembled embroidery. Other early examples, often with intricate patterns created with very fine yarns, have been found in Peruvian tombs. These were used to make splendid sets of clothes – and they were also used as wrappings for the dead. The dry atmosphere in both these countries has helped preserve these ancient textiles.

Illuminated manuscripts inspired weavers to create some of the wonderful Medieval tapestries that we can still see today. Later, it became more common for artists to produce painted designs which were then copied exactly by the weavers, giving the weavers much less freedom of interpretation. The original purpose of these large hangings was to cover cold stone walls, as well as being beautiful to look at.

Nowadays tapestry weaving is a popular art form, and although you can still find studios where huge tapestries are woven from artists' cartoons, there are also many artist-weavers who produce their own designs. Woven tapestries are strong and durable, and they look wonderful on walls, adding colour and a special feeling of warmth and comfort. Apart from wall hangings, you can weave floor rugs, cushions, bags, or even clothes. You can work with very fine yarns to produce miniature images, or with thick bundles of mixed fibres to create works on a giant scale. The basic techniques are common and all you need is a frame or simple loom to suit the size of the work.

Tapestry weaving can be totally absorbing. It is a wonderful contrast to the hustle and bustle of modern life and it feels good to handle natural materials like wool, cotton, flax and silk. People who see my work often say: 'You must have a lot of patience', but with the diversity of colours and textures of different yarns, each part of the weaving process offers an exciting challenge, and patience does not come into it. Once you have experienced the pleasure of weaving your first simple piece, I hope you will be inspired to go on to create your own designs.

MATERIALS

In tapestry weaving you construct the cloth at the same time as weaving the design, so you need to consider both the warp and the weft yarns before you start. The warp is attached to the frame or loom, and runs vertically through the tapestry. The weft is woven across the warp to build up the pattern.

WARP

The warp is the foundation of the tapestry. It has to be kept very tight while you work, so you will need a good strong yarn. I prefer a linen rug warp as it does not stretch, is firm and strong, and hangs well. However, it can be difficult to get the tension right, so cotton may be a better choice for a beginner. Tightly spun wool also makes a good warp material, and is lovely to work with. In traditional tapestry the warp is completely covered by the weft, so the colour of the warp is not important, but it is easier on the eyes to work with a pale, natural yarn, rather than with a dark one. A brightly coloured warp can look good, when knotted or fringed warp ends are part of the finished design.

The spacing of the warp depends on the thickness of the warp threads, and the amount of detail you want to include in your design. The finer the warp and weft, and the closer the warp threads are, the more detail will be possible, and of course the longer the weaving time.

WEFT

When it comes to the weft, the choice is endless, but as a basic rule the thickness of the weft should fit in the space between two warps. It is a good idea to start with a few plain rug yarns, then gradually build up a collection of materials. You can use anything from traditional embroidery yarns for a regular, fine weave to the thickest rug yarn. You can use silk, cotton, linen, and any type of wool or other fibres, either on their own or with several mixed together. Hand spun yarns can give lovely results. If you are a spinner, try using sheep's wool, dog hair, camel hair, and even your own hair.

If you like more texture and variety you can weave with absolutely anything that will bend enough to go over and under the warp. In workshops with children I have used rags, dustbin liners, raw fleece, silk waste, feathers, beads, strips of film, bubble wrap, pipe cleaners, and many other unlikely sounding materials, all to great effect.

Warp and weft yarns
The basket in the foreground holds skeins of wool for the weft. The basket at the top left has a mixture of fine linen and cotton that can either be used as weft yarns on their own for very fine work, or mixed, many strands together. On the right are reels of different types of warp yarns. You can purchase reels of warp yarn that are labelled with the recommended number of ends (warp threads) per centimetre (inch).

FRAME OR LOOM?

Warp threads must be stretched tightly to maintain an even weave up the length of the warp. All the project tapestries shown in this book were woven on simple rectangular frames with notches along the top and bottom edges, but purpose-built horizontal or vertical looms are more appropriate for large tapestries.

The simplest form of weaving frame is a piece of strong, stiff card. Although this type of frame can be used to good effect, I recommend the use of wooden frames as these allow you to make the warp very tight. You can buy ready-made frames in different sizes, but you could adapt an old picture frame.

The frame need only be slightly wider than the finished tapestry, but it should be at least 25cm (10in) longer. The extra length is necessary to allow for starter wefts and hems (see pages 20–21) and for general ease of weaving at the top of the tapestry.

The best way to work with a frame is to rest one end of it on a table, and the other end in your lap. The inset photograph shows two types of ready-made weaving frames: the wooden frame is similar to the one used for the projects in this book; the other is a simple rectangle of strong card.

This is a corner of my studio, showing my large upright tapestry loom with work in progress. The loom has beams at the top and bottom, and more warp can be exposed gradually from the top beam, as the finished work is wound round the bottom one. The baskets contain my different weft yarns which are sorted according to colour. Mixed butterflies of weft yarn (see page 18) can be seen loosely stuck into the warp. At the top of the loom is a large, flat wooden stick, woven through the warp to make one shed (an opening in the warp through which the weft is passed), and below it a metal bar with string heddles used to pull out the second shed.

OTHER WEAVING EQUIPMENT

Tape measure   Use this to position the warp centrally on the frame, and to check the width of the weaving from time to time.

Scissors   Make sure you have sharp scissors to cut threads while working, and to cut the tapestry off the frame at the end.

Bobbins   For spacing out warp threads evenly.

Shed stick   Flat wooden stick inserted through the warp to make the shed. If the warp becomes loose, tighten it by weaving in more sticks and pushing them to the top.

Paper and pencil   For drawing and colouring designs.

Felt-tipped pens   Used to mark the outlines of designs on the warp.

Wooden dowel or bamboo   For hanging the finished piece.

Beads, feathers, small lengths of bamboo   To decorate the warp ends of the finished piece.

Needles   To stitch the hem to the back, and to sew in ends that show on the front.

Some people like to weave with a needle or a bobbin with the weft yarn wound round it. I prefer to use my fingers, and work with a butterfly (see page 18). That way I have maximum contact with the materials, and it is easier to keep the weaving even.

12

MOUNTING AND FRAMING EQUIPMENT

Blockboard   For mounting the tapestry prior to framing.

PVA glue   For securing a tapestry to blockboard.

Wooden strips   To construct a simple frame.

Sandpaper   For rubbing down the edges of the frame.

Hammer and nails   To assemble the frame around the blockboard.

Hardboard   Used to set the blockboard in from the front edge of the wooden frame.

Acrylic paints and paint brush   To paint the frame.

Awl and eye screws   To complete the frame

Apron and gloves   I try to keep the paints well away from the textiles, and always wear gloves and an apron when I am painting the wooden frames.

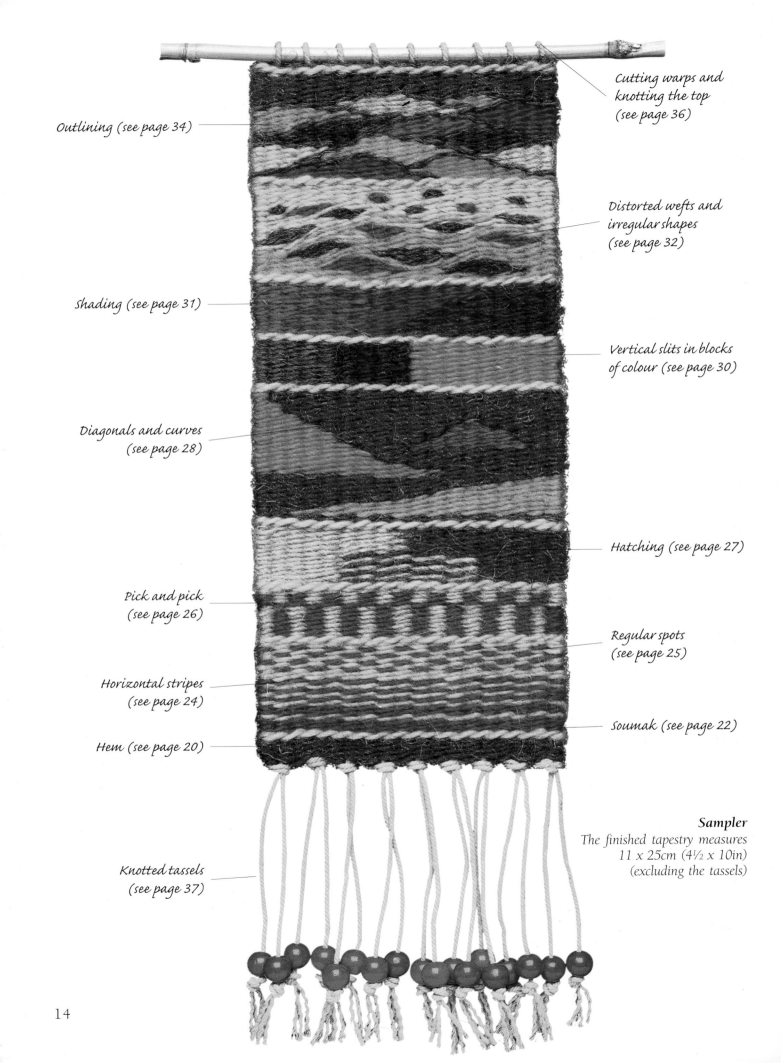

Outlining (see page 34)

Cutting warps and
knotting the top
(see page 36)

Distorted wefts and
irregular shapes
(see page 32)

Shading (see page 31)

Vertical slits in blocks
of colour (see page 30)

Diagonals and curves
(see page 28)

Hatching (see page 27)

Pick and pick
(see page 26)

Regular spots
(see page 25)

Horizontal stripes
(see page 24)

Hem (see page 20)

Soumak (see page 22)

Knotted tassels
(see page 37)

Sampler
*The finished tapestry measures
11 x 25cm (4½ x 10in)
(excluding the tassels)*

BASIC TECHNIQUES

The sampler opposite contains some of the most useful basic tapestry weaving techniques, and by combining these in different ways you will be able to weave a wide range of designs.

On the following pages, I show you how to work all the different techniques – you can either weave the complete sampler as shown, or pick out smaller areas to concentrate on specific techniques. If you have already done some weaving you may chose to move straight on to another design, and use the sampler for reference only.

At the bottom of the sampler is a short hem that makes a base for the tapestry. This is followed by blocks of different techniques, separated by rows of soumak knotting.

Horizontal stripes and **regular spots** are worked across the full width of the warp, and both can be used for shading by varying the distance between them. **Pick and pick** is also worked across the full width of the warp and makes regular vertical stripes. **Hatching** is very effective, and easy to do once you have got the hang of it. **Diagonal lines and curves** are made by stepping the weaving, as if you were drawing them on graph paper. **Blocks of colour** worked across part of the warp make vertical slits, which can be left open, or dealt with in a variety of ways. The technique of **shading** is very similar to that for hatching.

The weft is worked as straight lines, at right-angles to the warp, for all the above techniques. However, in the last two sections – **irregular shapes** and **outlining** – the weaving becomes freer, and the weft is built up in some places and runs across the warp at different angles to create an interesting surface.

When the weaving is finished, the warp is cut off the frame, and the warp ends at the top and bottom are knotted so that the weaving cannot unravel. For this sampler I cut the warp to leave short ends at the top and long ends at the bottom. I then added a length of bamboo at the top to hang it from, and a row of beads at the bottom to decorate the tassels.

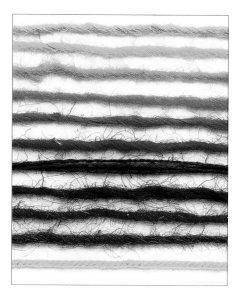

I used quite a thick, bright yellow cotton yarn (bottom) for the warp and a range of single-ply rug wools for the weft.

WINDING WARPS

Before winding a warp, you must decide on the size of the tapestry and the types of yarn you want to use for the warp and the weft. These factors affect the number of threads you include in the warp.

The relationship between the warp and the weft is very important – as a general rule, the weft should fit easily in the gap between the warps. If the weft yarn is too thick it may not cover the warp, whereas if the weft yarn is too thin, it will make the weaving very slow, and it will be rather difficult to build up shapes.

The number of warp threads wound across the width of the warp affects both the detail and texture in the finished tapestry. The greater the number of warp threads over a given width, the smoother and more detailed the design will be. Winding various widths of warp with different warp yarns (see page 50) and then weaving test pieces is a good way of learning how all these factors affect the finished piece.

Tapestry weaving is not an exact science; measurements are never really accurate (they will vary from person to person), so those given in this book are intended only as a guide. The spacing of the notches on warping frames, for example, varies from brand to brand, and this will affect the width of the warp.

Having decided on the width of the tapestry, I wind the warp with my chosen yarn, placing one thread in each notch. I then look at the relationship between the weft yarns and the warp threads. If I need a few more threads than there are notches, I wind double threads round some of the notches (spacing them evenly across the width of the warp), then use the starter weft (see page 20) to equalise the spacing between each thread. The diagrams below show how I would set up the same warp on different frames.

If you need a fine warp yarn, you can wind multiple threads in each notch (see page 59), or combine both the top and bottom layers of the warp (see page 55).

For the sampler shown on page 14, I used a thick cotton yarn for the warp, winding 18 threads across 11cm (4½in) of the frame. This is quite an open warp but it works well with the chosen weft yarns. It is ideal for practising the basic techniques and makes the step-by-step photographs quite easy to follow.

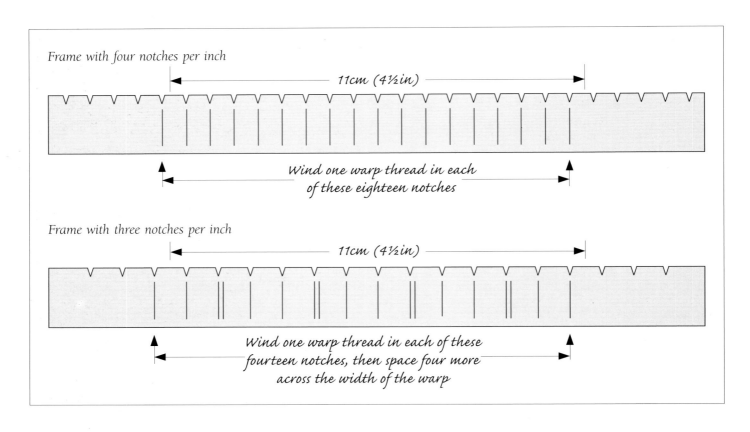

Frame with four notches per inch

11cm (4½in)

Wind one warp thread in each of these eighteen notches

Frame with three notches per inch

11cm (4½in)

Wind one warp thread in each of these fourteen notches, then space four more across the width of the warp

1. Make pencil marks, either side of the centre of the top of the frame, against the notches closest to the required width of the tapestry. Repeat the marks along the bottom edge. When you start weaving, this side of the frame should be facing you.

2. Wind the warp thread round the notch at the start point at the top of the frame, make a single knot and pull the thread tight.

3. Take the warp thread down to the corresponding notch at the bottom of the frame, pull it tight, and then clamp it with your thumb.

4. Now take the warp thread up the back of the frame and locate it in the next notch.

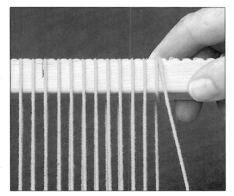

5. Keeping the thread tight, repeat steps 3 and 4 until you have eighteen warps on the front of the frame, and the end of the thread is back at the knotted end of the frame. Trim to leave a 15cm (6in) tail. Wind this tail two or three times round the frame.

6. Turn the frame over and tie the loose end of the thread securely to the last warp with two half-hitches.

PREPARING WEFT YARNS

For this sampler I used single strands of rug yarn for the weft, but you could work with two or more finer yarns together to make up the required thickness, or to blend in different shades.

Whether you work with one strand or more, it is a good idea to make a 'butterfly' for each weft colour. Butterflies keeps the weft yarns in order and stop them from getting tangled. They are also easier to weave with than long loose lengths.

Most of my yarns come in skeins, so before making butterflies for weaving with, I use a swift and a ball winder. The swift (the adjustable spool at the right of this picture) holds the skein, and allows it to unwind without tangling.

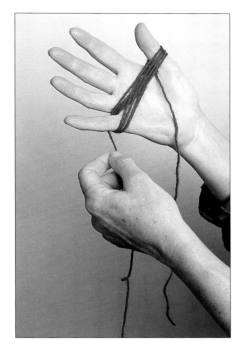

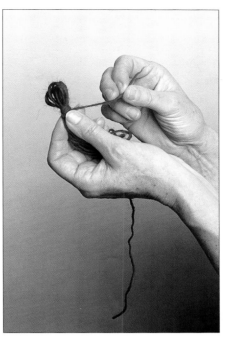

1. To make a butterfly, hook one end of the yarn round your thumb, leaving a 20cm (8in) tail hanging, then wind ten figure-of-eight loops round your thumb and little finger.

2. Carefully remove the weft yarn from your thumb and finger, cut the end to about 10cm (4in), wind this end several times round the top loop, then secure it with a half-hitch knot.

You can bring together two, three or more shades or thicknesses of yarn to make mixed butterflies. Try to make up each weft to the same thickness.

To test a weft, twist the yarns gently together, and place them lengthwise between two warps; they should fill the gap quite snugly. If they look too bulky, take out a few threads. On the other hand, if they look too thin, add a few more threads.

Butterflies ready to weave the sampler.

When the free end of the butterfly gets too short to work with, hold the knotted end and pull out a loop of yarn from the butterfly.

WEAVING THE HEM

The hem is the base of a tapestry. It spaces out the warp threads evenly, and gives you a firm foundation to work on. It can be unravelled when the tapestry is finished, before the warp ends are knotted, or it can be turned under and stitched to the back of the tapestry.

Make sure you lay in enough weft yarn to cover the warps completely, and try to keep the tension even. If you lay the weft in too tightly, it will pull in the sides of the warp, and the tapestry will look flat. On the other hand, if there is too much weft in each row the tapestry will bulge and get wider, and the warp ribs will stand out. Check that you have a nice straight edge across the hem before you start the actual weaving.

1. Turn the frame so that the knotted ends of the warp threads are at the top, then, as we are working with just the top set of warp threads, place a thin sheet of cardboard on top of the bottom set. This hides the bottom set of warp threads, and makes it easier to see what you are doing.

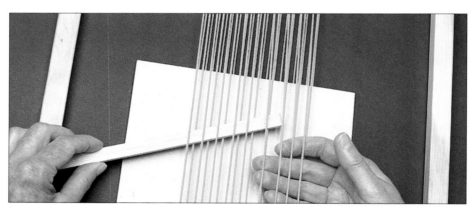

2. Starting from the left, weave a shed stick under the first warp then over and under the rest.

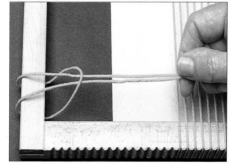

3. Create a starter weft. Cut a length of the warp yarn three times the full width of the frame, fold it in half and loop it round one side of the frame.

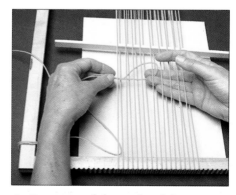

4. Pass one of the ends of the starter weft through the same shed as the shed stick, then push it down loosely to the bottom of the frame.

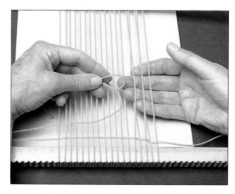

5. Pick up the alternate set of warp threads and weave the other starter weft through these.

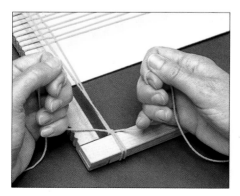

6. Take the ends of both starter wefts round the right-hand side of the frame, pull them very tight, and then secure with a reef knot.

7. Use a bobbin to push the starter wefts down the warps to form a straight line across the warp. Neaten and equalise the space between each warp thread.

8. Start the first row of the hem by taking the weft butterfly *under* the first warp thread on the left. Pick up two or three warp threads at a time, then pass the butterfly under these.

9. Continue picking more warp threads and passing the weft yarn through to the other side of the warp. Leave the weft quite loose.

10. Use the tips of your fingers to push the weft yarn down on to the starter weft.

11. On the second row, pass the butterfly through the first few warp threads of the other shed. Hold the right-hand warp, then gently pull the loop of the weft up against it.

12. Weave the weft yarn across to the other side of the warp, then push it down with your fingers.

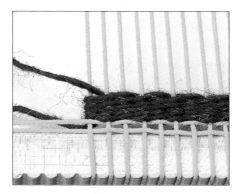

13. Continue the hem until you have woven ten rows. Push the weft down firmly every few rows to ensure that the warp is completely covered.

14. Take the weft under the last warp (it is now under the last two warp threads) then make a half hitch round the last warp.

15. Pull the knot closed then trim off the excess weft thread.

KNOTTING A SOUMAK

A row of soumak knots creates a slightly raised line across the warp. The weft is wrapped around each warp thread instead of passing through the shed. I have used rows of soumak to separate the different blocks of pattern for this sampler.

When I want to fold under the hem (see pages 39 and 66), I include a row of soumak between the hem and the weaving itself as the bulkiness of knotting covers the warp that would otherwise be exposed on the fold.

Soumak can be worked from either side. I find it easier to work left to right, but if you want to work the other way, just reverse the action. Consecutive rows of soumak, knotted alternately from either side of the warp can create an interesting texture (see page 39).

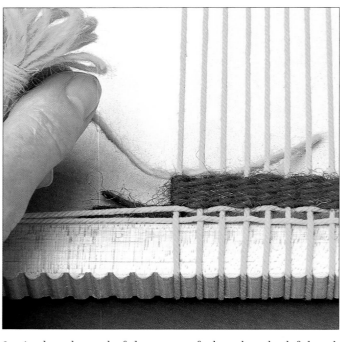

1. Anchor the end of the new weft thread at the left-hand side of the frame by taking it under, over and under the last three warps.

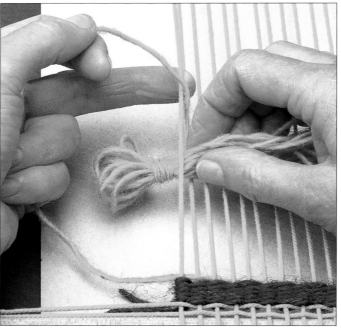

2. Pick up the left-hand warp with a finger, then pass the weft butterfly under this thread from the right.

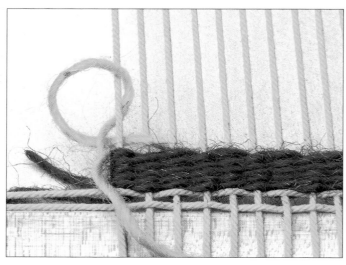

3. Bring the weft out through the loop, then gently pull the weft yarn towards you to close the knot around the first warp thread.

4. Push the closed knot down to the hem.

5. Repeat steps 2-4 to make another knot around the second warp thread.

It is a good idea to check the width of your weaving from time to time. If it starts to get narrower you must put in a little more weft across each row (to slacken the tension slightly), without letting the edges get too loose.

6. Continue knotting round each warp until you reach the other side of the tapestry.

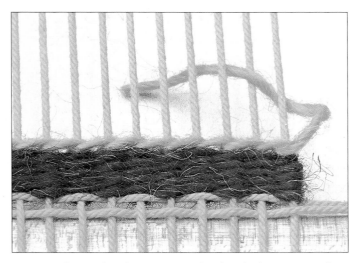

7. Trim the end to leave a 5cm (2in) tail, then weave this back, taking it under, over and under three warps threads.

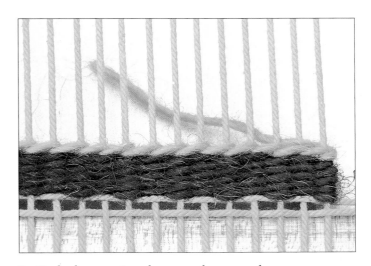

8. Push the weaving down to the soumak.

HORIZONTAL STRIPES AND SPOTS

To create a solid horizontal stripe of colour across the warp you must weave at least two rows of the same colour, one in each shed, then follow this with at least two rows of a second colour.

To create a broken line (spots of colour) you must weave a single row of one colour, then follow this with at least two rows of a second colour. Weaving an even number of rows of yellow between single rows of red will create staggered spots of red as shown in step 10. However, if you weave an odd number of rows of yellow between single rows of red, you will create vertical columns of yellow spots.

1. Referring to steps 8–12 on page 21, and starting at the left-hand side of the warp, weave six rows of red. Leave the red butterfly on the left.

2. Join the yellow at the right-hand side of the warp. In this case the weft needs to cover the first warp, so instead of weaving it over, and leaving the end loose on top, start it with a half hitch round the first warp (the free end naturally tucks under the warp, and does not have to be sewn in afterwards).

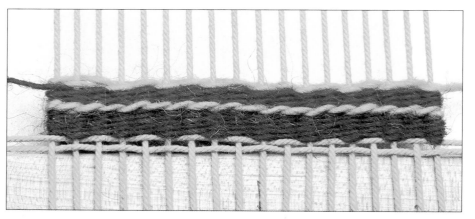

3. Weave two rows of yellow, leaving the butterfly at the right-hand side.

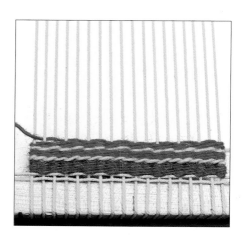

4. Pick up the red weft and weave another four rows, leaving the butterfly on the left-hand side.

5. Continue weaving horizontal lines of alternating colours: at this stage I have woven another six rows – two of yellow, two of red and two more of yellow. When a weft runs out bring the tail to the front, lay in a new butterfly with the two tails in adjacent gaps. Continue weaving in the same direction with the new butterfly to the end of the row . . .

6. . . . then push both tails down through the same gap to the back.

7. Push the weft down, then take the red weft back across the weaving. Finish this section of horizontal lines with four rows of yellow.

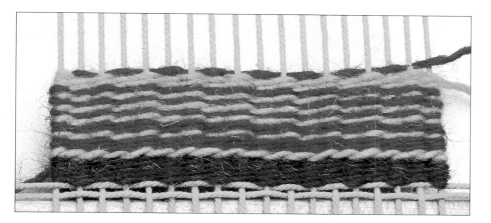 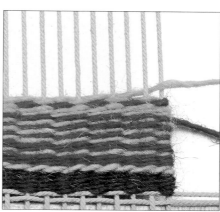

8. Start the spots by taking the red weft under the first warp at the left-hand side and weaving a single row across to the right-hand side.

9. Take the yellow weft over the red one, then weave two rows, ending back at the right-hand side.

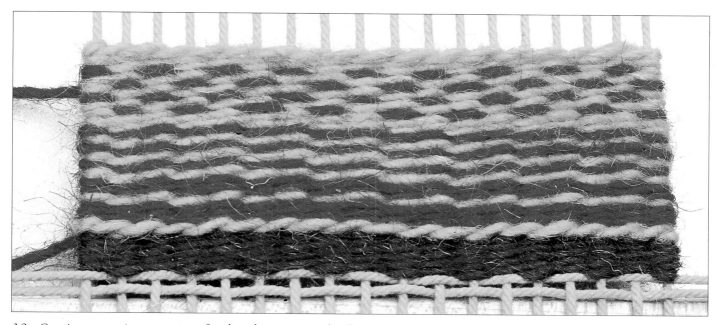

10. Continue weaving one row of red and two rows of yellow. Notice how the spots are visible on alternating sheds. Complete this section of the sampler with a row of soumak (see page 22).

PICK AND PICK

Weaving one row of one colour followed by one row of another, and repeating that sequence will create vertical stripes. This technique always makes the edges a little awkward to weave, as the two colours have to be twisted around each other to make sure they cover the end warp threads.

Pick and pick can be worked with contrasting colours to create definite stripes as in this sampler, or with more subtle shades where the stripes hardly show as in the mask on page 5.

1. Weave a row of red weft across the warp ending at the right-hand side. Referring to step 2 on page 24, start a yellow weft in the opposite shed at the left-hand side, and weave this across to the right-hand side.

2. Loop the red weft round the right-hand warp, take it under the first two warp threads, then weave it across to the left-hand side.

3. Weave the yellow across to the left – it should finish on top of the last warp. Bring the red over the yellow and start to weave it back across the warp.

4. Hold the yellow then pull the red to draw the loop in at the left.

5. Complete the row of red then weave the yellow across to the right-hand side.

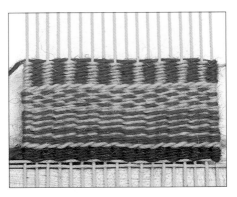

6. Continue working in this way until you have seven rows of yellow and eight rows of red, finishing with the yellow butterfly at the right-hand side and the red at the left.

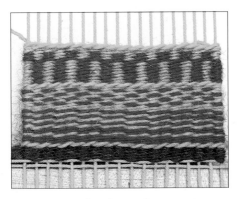

7. Reverse the design by weaving a second row of red then alternating the colours for a few more rows. End with the yellow weft on the left-hand side, then work a row of soumak to finish this section (see page 22).

HATCHING

For this technique two colours are worked together so that they dovetail into each other. You can make the overlaps long or short. For this technique to work the two weft colours must be woven towards each other in one shed, and away from each other in the opposite shed (see also shading on page 31). The is the one rule of tapestry weaving that must be obeyed.

1. Weave the yellow from the left-hand side to the fifth warp, then back to the left. Start a blue butterfly on the right, and weave this across till you get to where the yellow turned. Weave blue back to the right-hand side. Next weave yellow to within five warps of the right-hand side, then back to the left. Weave blue across to where the yellow turned then back to the right-hand side. In this photograph, I have left the weave open to show the structure more clearly. In practice, you would push the weaving down after each row.

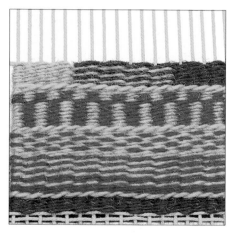

2. Continue the pattern of weaving as step 1, working two part-rows with each colour in turn.

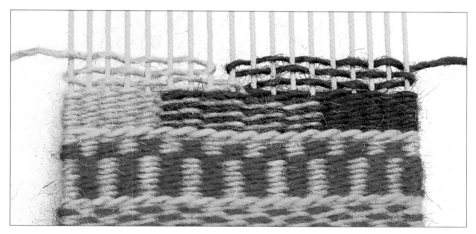

3. Now, work the yellow and blue together to the middle of the warp and take them back to their respective sides. Weave the yellow across and back again, stopping it one warp thread short of the previous row. Weave the blue across and back again, taking it one warp past the previous blue row. Again, I have left the weave open in this photograph.

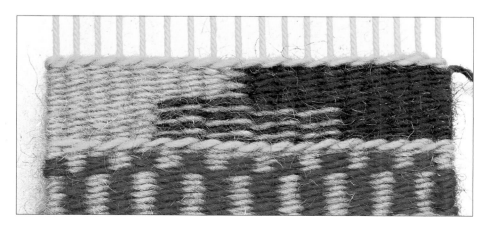

4. Continue the pattern of weaving as step 3, working two part-rows with each colour in turn. Trim the yellow to leave a 5cm (2in) tail, but leave the blue butterfly at the right-hand side. Again, finish this section of the sampler with another row of soumak (see page 22).

DIAGONAL SHAPES AND CURVES

Diagonals in weaving are formed by stepping the weft: shallow steps form an acute diagonal; taller steps form a steeper one. You can weave the shapes either side of the diagonal separately, but you must weave the decreasing shape first so it forms a base for the adjoining area.

Curves are also made by stepping the weft, but you gradually increase the depth of each step. See page 47 for details about weaving circles.

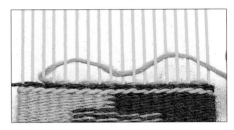

1. Start this section with three rows of blue. Then, working from the right-hand side, lay in a row of orange, taking it across to the third warp from the left and back again.

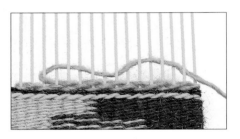

2. Now weave the orange across until it is two warps short of the previous row, and back again.

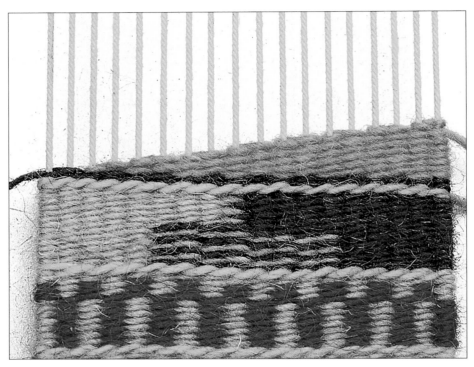

3. Continue weaving with the orange, reducing the width by two warp threads on each row. Finish with a half hitch at the right-hand side, then trim the weft to leave a 5cm (2in) tail.

4. Now work the open area with the blue weft, stepping it to match the orange shape. When it is level with the top of the orange leave the blue butterfly at the right-hand side.

5. Start the second shade of orange on the left, weaving it to within seven warps of the right-hand side and back again. Continue weaving across and back again five times, reducing the width by one warp on each row.

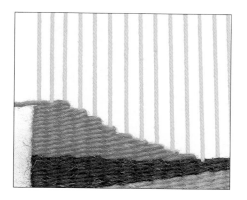

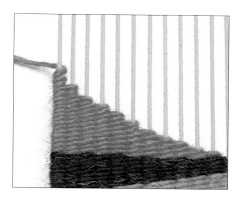

6. Increase the angle of the weave, by working two rows round the same warp. Weave three more sets of double rows, reducing the width by one warp on each pair.

7. Weave three rows on the last two warps, then finish the curve by wrapping the weft three times round the last warp.

8. Weave some rows of the blue background colour, turning back when each row meets the orange. Leave the blue yarn at the left-hand side, then lay in a brown yarn through seven warp threads for the start of a triangular shape, and a separate blue for the right-hand fill.

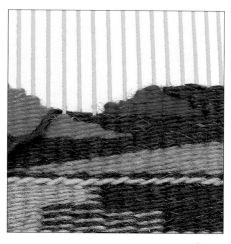

9. Weave a triangle with the brown yarn, stepping in on both sides by one warp thread every two rows. Use the new blue yarn to fill in the area on the right-hand side of the triangle.

10. Use the original blue yarn to fill in the area at the left-hand side of the brown triangle, then work the remaining area to match the orange shape on the left. When the top of the section is straight and level, add a row of soumak (see page 22).

VERTICAL SLITS

If you weave blocks of colour that begin or end at the same warp, you will end up with a slit. If the slit is quite short, it is possible to leave it open. In the mask and hands weaving on page 5, I left the long slits between the fingers open and I pulled the weft for the finger tight to exaggerate the effect.

If you do not want the slits to show you can interlock the two areas by weaving one colour into the other at intervals (similar to the hatching on page 27) or, for a clean line, you can stitch up the slit with a fine thread.

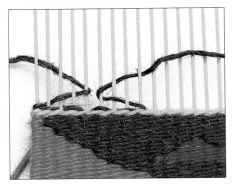

1. Working with the nine warps to the left of centre, lay in a purple and a green yarn, then weave a couple of rows of each colour, turning back at the same gap in the warp.

2. Link the purple into the green at intervals, and continue until they measure approximately 2cm (¾in).

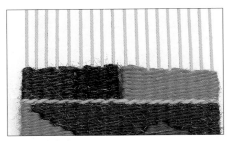

3. Now fill in the right-hand side of the warp with a block of orange, without linking it to the purple.

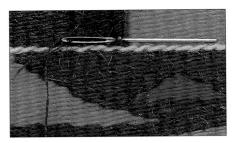

4. Thread a strand of fine cotton thread in a large needle, then take the needle down under the right-hand warp in the block of purple weaving and back up through the slit between the purple and orange.

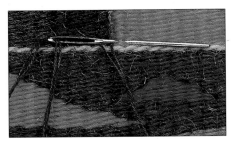

5. Thread the other end of the cotton through the eye of the needle (the cotton is now looped round the warp and ready to be used double). Take the needle down through the centre slit and up round the left-hand warp of the orange block.

6. Continue sewing up the slit, working in a figure-of-eight round the two end warps. At the top of the slit, weave the cotton through two warps, and tie it off with a reef knot round a warp thread. Trim the excess cotton then tuck the ends between two warps to the back of the warp.

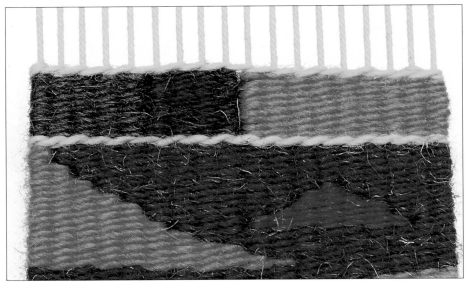

7. Finish the section with another row of soumak (see page 22).

SHADING

This technique is very similar to that for hatching (see page 27), but a little more random. Weaving two similar tones of colour together will create subtle shading, whereas working two contrasting tones together produces a more distinct shading. I used three colours in the sampler: orange, red and purple. The orange and red illustrate subtle shading, and the red and purple a more distinct shading.

For this technique to work, it is important to lay each colour of weft yarn into the warp correctly (see hatching on page 27).

1. Lay in the three colours as shown. They must all lie in the same shed, with tails and heads together in the start position.

2. Take the red and purple tails to the back (here, they pass through the gap between the seventh and eighth warp threads from the right-hand side), then start to weave. The colours take turns to overlap each other, and you work two rows of each colour before moving on to the next one. In this photograph, I have opened out the weft to show its structure, but you should push the weft down every few rows.

3. Continue building up the section until it measures 2cm (¾in), then add a row of soumak (see page 22).

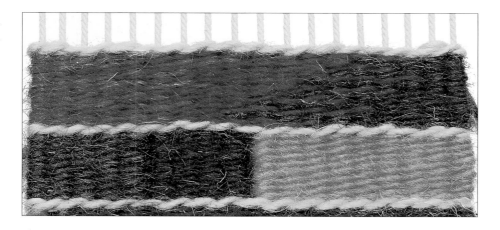

DISTORTED WEFT

In all the previous techniques the weft was woven in straight lines at right-angles to the warp. This method of weaving is suitable for simple designs such as those on pages 43 and 45. However, you can create a different type of texture, and achieve a lively and interesting surface by building the weft up in some areas, and weaving it at different angles to the warp. This type of weaving needs a little more weft yarn laid into each row to cover the warp properly, and it does become a little harder to keep the edges straight, and the weaving flat.

Distorted wefts are woven at random so it is difficult to give accurate step-by-step instructions. Remember that this is only a sampler and you do not have to copy my design exactly. Weave a few lozenge shapes as shown here and then try experimenting with other shapes.

1. Work three rows of orange yarn to create a base for this section, then work a lozenge shape with purple yarn. Here, I have left the weft open to show the way the shape starts on one warp and gradually grows to five warps, before getting smaller again. The inset photograph shows the same shape pushed flat.

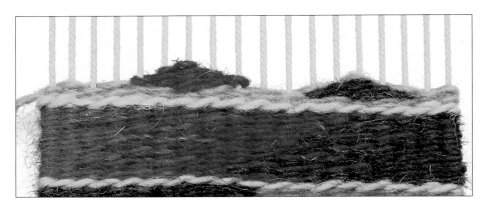

2. Weave a row of orange across the top of the purple lozenge (from right to left) following the shape of the lozenge. Now weave another lozenge with red yarn in a similar way to the purple one.

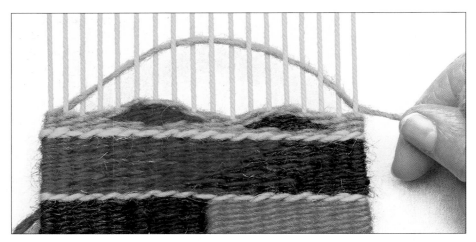

3. Weave three rows of orange, pushing the weft down on to the contours of the two shapes after each row.

4. Now weave a green lozenge shape in the dip between the other two.

5. Continue working up the warp, placing the shapes at random, and weaving the background colour between. Gradually reduce the size of the lozenge shapes from five warps to four, and then three, and introduce yellow to the background. To weave random spots on just one warp thread, wind a short length of weft yarn twice round an exposed warp thread and pull the loops down as shown in the inset detail.

6. To avoid the red spot becoming lost in the background, pass the background weft yarn under the warp with the spot on it – note that the weft passes under three warps.

7. Bring the background yarn back across the warp (in this shed the yellow yarn will automatically pass under the warp with the spot on).

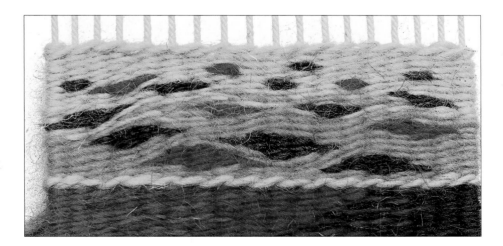

8. Continue the weaving, adding a few more lozenge shapes and spots at random, and working the yellow in different areas until the top of the weft is horizontal. Finally, add a row of soumak (see page 22).

33

OUTLINING SHAPES

Horizontal shapes tend to blend into each other and get lost, but if you want them to show up more, they can be outlined with a contrasting colour. Outlining can also help to smooth down a shape and give a diagonal or curved edge a less stepped look.

Remember that one row of the contrast colour will make a dotted outline and two rows a solid one.

1. Lay in a red yarn, then weave a simple shape (see inset), bearing in mind that its depth will be much smaller when the weft is pushed down.

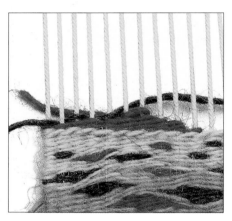

2. Lay in a green weft, in the same shed as the last row of red, and weave it across to the left-hand side of the red shape.

3. Weave the green yarn across the top of the red shape and turn it back one warp past the end of the shape.

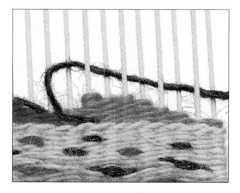

4. Weave an orange shape so that it overlaps the green outline by two warps, then work the green weft across the top of the shape.

5. Weave the green yarn back to its start point, then push it down to follow the contours of the shapes.

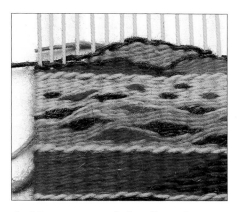

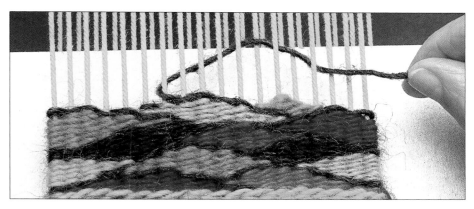

6. Now weave a dark yellow shape in the middle of the warp and outline this shape with the green.

7. Continue weaving and outlining random shapes in different colours. Here I am about to cover the small dark yellow shape. Two rows of green have already been worked across the pale yellow shape so, to keep the outline at an even thickness, the weft is taken under five warps then woven across the yellow.

8. Bring the green weft back across the dark yellow shape, then take the end through to the back of the warp.

9. When the last shape has been outlined in green, lay in a blue yarn at the left-hand side and start weaving the background colour.

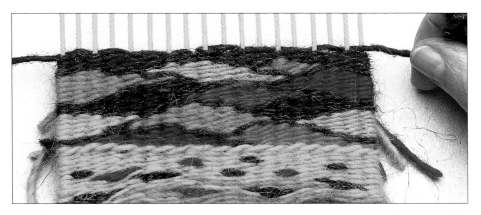

10. Start another blue yarn in the centre, where the green yarn ended, then fill in the dips at the right-hand side. When the weft is straight and horizontal, use one butterfly to weave another six rows.

11. Add a row of soumak, then weave two more rows of blue, ending with a half hitch round the last warp.

CUTTING THE TAPESTRY FROM THE FRAME

When you have finished weaving your tapestry, it must be cut from the frame. I always find this a really exciting moment – whether I have been doing a miniature piece, or a huge hanging. It is the moment when the weaving becomes a piece of work in its own right.

This sampler is designed as a small wall hanging, so a length of bamboo is inserted at the top of the weaving to provide a rigid support. The tapestry is then cut from the frame and the top lengths of warp threads knotted round the bamboo. Finally, the bottom warp threads are knotted and decorated with beads.

1. Remove the shed stick, then weave a length of bamboo through the opposite shed of warp threads.

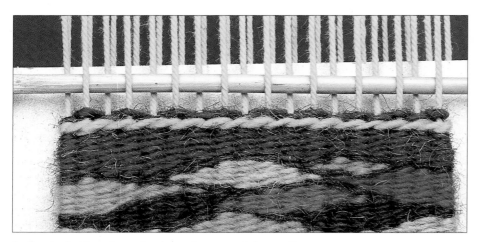

2. Push the bamboo down to the top of the weft.

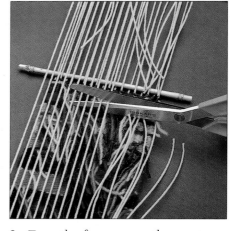

3. Turn the frame over, then cut through the warp threads on the back of the frame.

4. Fold the cut warp threads out of the way, then cut the starter weft threads at the bottom of the tapestry.

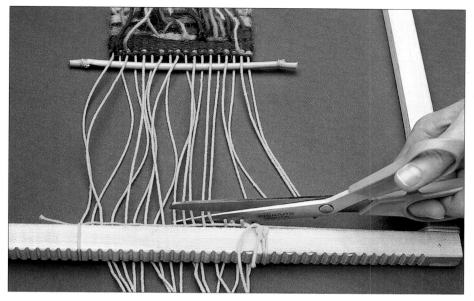

5. Cut through the warp threads above the bamboo, then lift the tapestry off the frame.

6. Place the tapestry face down on the work surface and place a weight on top. Tie pairs of warp threads round the bamboo using reef knots. Tie the two sides first, then work across the tapestry.

7. Trim off the excess warp threads at the top of the tapestry, then trim the tails of the weft threads on the back of the tapestry to about 2.5cm (1in).

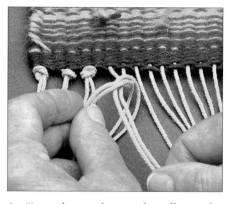

8. Turn the work round, pull out the starter weft threads at the bottom of the work, then make overhand knots with pairs of warp threads . . .

9. . . . then use your thumb to push the knots tight up against the bottom of the tapestry.

10. Thread a bead on each warp thread, form a double knot . . .

11. . . . then pull the knot tight. Continue across the warp, ensuring that the beads and their knots are parallel to the bottom of the tapestry. Finally, trim the tassels to length.

OTHER WAYS OF FINISHING WARP ENDS

The simple knotting of the top round a length of bamboo, and the beaded tassels shown on the previous page is just one method of finishing the warp ends. There are many other decorative finishes, however, that can add interest to a design, and here are a few possibilities to consider.

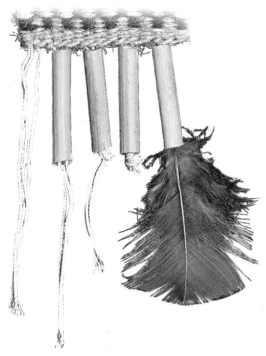

Bamboo and feather tassels

This tassel is used for the *Peruvian Birds* tapestry shown on page 43. This photograph shows the step-by-step sequence. Thread two or three warp ends through a length of hollow bamboo. Tie an overhand knot. Trim the warp ends slightly shorter than the length of bamboo. Thread the warp ends back through the bamboo leaving the knot at the end. Push a feather into the bamboo and arrange it so that it covers the knot. Repeat across the width of the warp. Note that in the finished tapestry, eight tassels have three warps ends in each, and three have two warp ends.

Knotted tassels

These tassels were used for the three different sizes of tapestry shown on page 51. To link the white tassels to the finished tapestry I used the warp yarn to weave a short hem and to knot a row of soumak. When the weaving was cut from the frame, I knotted pairs of warp ends together, then, working with each warp end alternately, I knotted a series of half hitches to create the knotted tassel. I finished with an overhand knot, then trimmed off the excess threads.

Wrapped tassels

This tassel forms part of the *Cat and Fishes* shown on page 45. Knot sets of three warp ends together with an overhand knot and push the knot tight up against the bottom of the tapestry. Wrap one of the weft yarns tightly round the three warp ends. Make another overhand knot at the bottom of the wrapping, then trim off the excess warp thread.

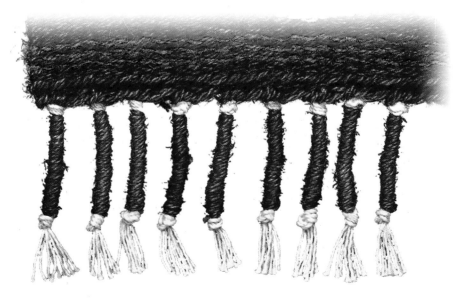

Woven block tassels

For the tassels on the bottom of this test piece, I used the vertical slits technique (see page 30) when weaving the hem. I wove small blocks of different colours over four warps, then linked the tops of these together with two full rows of dark blue hem. I then worked three rows of soumak, knotting the first and third rows from the left-hand side and the second from the right-hand side. When the tapestry was cut off the frame, I tied together the four warp ends in each block of colour with an overhand knot, pushing the knot tight up against its block of colour to form the pointed shape.

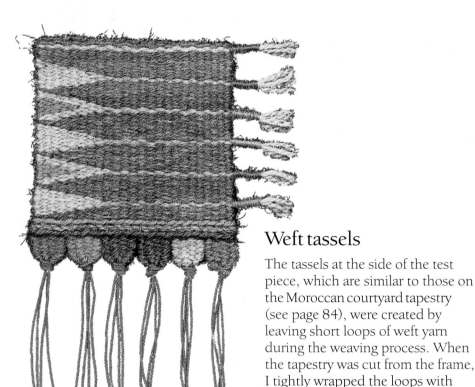

Weft tassels

The tassels at the side of the test piece, which are similar to those on the Moroccan courtyard tapestry (see page 84), were created by leaving short loops of weft yarn during the weaving process. When the tapestry was cut from the frame, I tightly wrapped the loops with weft yarn then cut through the small loops at the end.

Twisted tassels

This is a very simple yet effective form of tassel. Pairs of warp ends are tied together with an overhand knot, then the two warps are both twisted separately (in the same direction as their natural twist) until they twist round each other. Hold the end of the twisted warp ends and secure the twist with another overhand knot. Trim off the excess warp ends.

Folding hems under

If you do not want to include tassels, you can fold the hems under and sew them to the back of the tapestry as shown here. This photograph shows a tapestry being prepared for mounting (see page 66).

SUN SAMPLER

The aim of this sampler was to get as many techniques as possible into one piece, but to still end up with an interesting design. It incorporates all the techniques shown on the previous pages.

I worked on a natural linen warp, spacing 76 warp threads across 38cm (15in) of the frame. I used single-ply rug yarns for most of the weft, but I also included some handspun, natural wool, cotton yarns and metallic threads.

I started the piece with the smallest unit of one warp, working the pick and pick technique with black and white yarn. Then, still using black and white, I worked alternating, small square blocks of colour over five warps for each.

After that, I doubled the size of the squares and worked different colours and techniques in each new section, finishing each with rows of soumak.

Working upwards, I doubled the size of the blocks again, then worked two areas of shading before ending with an extravagant orange sun at the top.

The slits between the small squares at the bottom were left open, but I stitched up those in the larger squares at the top.

I finished the top of the sampler with a turned-under hem, and wrapped the warp ends two and two at the bottom, finishing each pair off with a feather.

Metallic threads, cotton yarns, handspun, natural wool and single-ply rug yarns were used for the weft of this sampler. The warp was wound with a natural linen yarn (bottom).

Detail of the bottom section of the sampler opposite.

41

PERUVIAN BIRDS

When you have mastered the basic techniques, you might like to try this bird design, which I adapted from a piece of Peruvian, pre-Inca cloth. It consists of straight lines and diagonals and is quite easy to weave.

For this tapestry, I decided to use 30 medium weight cotton warps, spaced across 12cm (4¾in) of the frame. For the weft, I chose natural coloured wool for the background (you could mix two slightly different shades, or add a fine textured linen thread when you make up your butterflies), and a mixture of green and turquoise wool for the birds and symbols (I used several strands of fine knitting wool).

Having enlarged the diagram, I transferred the design on to the warp (see page 56). I started weaving with a row of soumak, a few rows of plain weaving and a border of pick and pick. I then worked up the design, introducing new colours where needed, and working each area separately.

I formed the birds' legs by wrapping weft yarn round one warp as shown on page 33. I used some hatching in the bodies and wings – you can leave the short slits open, but weave the green into the background at intervals where indicated in the diagram.

When the tapestry was cut from the frame, I knotted the top warp ends round a length of bamboo (see page 37) then formed the tassels as shown on page 38.

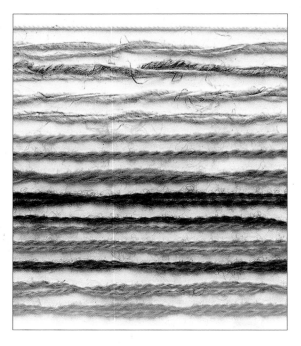

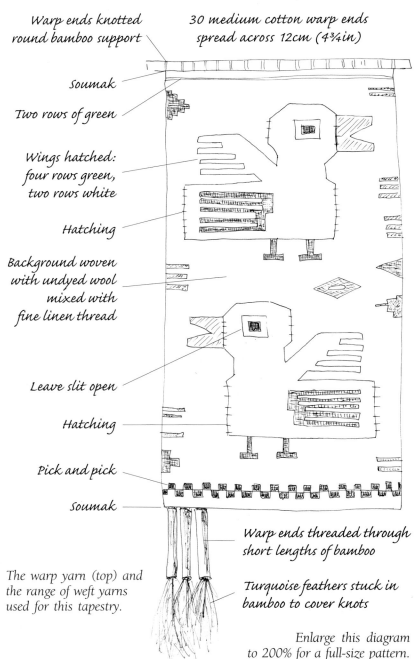

Warp ends knotted round bamboo support

30 medium cotton warp ends spread across 12cm (4¾in)

Soumak

Two rows of green

Wings hatched: four rows green, two rows white

Hatching

Background woven with undyed wool mixed with fine linen thread

Leave slit open

Hatching

Pick and pick

Soumak

Warp ends threaded through short lengths of bamboo

Turquoise feathers stuck in bamboo to cover knots

Enlarge this diagram to 200% for a full-size pattern.

The warp yarn (top) and the range of weft yarns used for this tapestry.

> *Do not let your pattern rule your weaving. I only use a pattern as a rough guide and, sometimes, if I feel that the weaving does not look right, I change it a little. Remember to build up your shapes slightly taller than you want them, so they do not end up looking squashed.*

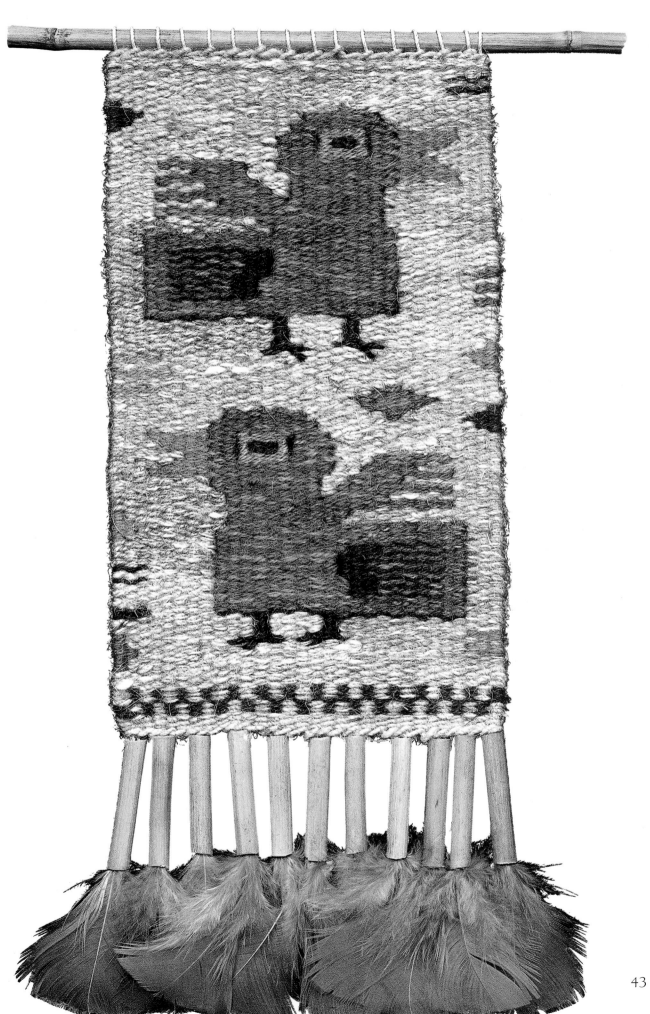

43

CAT AND FISHES

I find looking at ancient textiles a great inspiration and, although I never copy them directly, they can be a good starting point for a design. Like the birds on page 42, this stylised cat often appears in South American woven textiles. I found the symmetrical birds in an old cross-stitch sampler, and you can see fish, similar to these in textiles all over the world, where they have different symbolic meanings. Although there are several different styles and creatures crammed into a small space, the design works well, because it is simple, and uses only a few colours.

I used 33 medium cotton warp ends, spaced out to 14cm (5½in) across the frame.

I chose two shades of blue wool for the background, and two shades of white cotton for the creatures. The white wefts consist of five strands of very fine, quite roughly spun cotton with tiny multicoloured flecks in them. I also used small amounts of red and orange wool to liven things up a bit.

Having transferred the design on to the warp (see page 56) I wove the design, introducing new colours where needed.

At the top of the design I wove in a length of bamboo, then added six rows of blue. It can be difficult to make the weaving above the bamboo look neat, so you could weave the six rows of blue higher up the warp, then push them down to the bamboo afterwards.

Having cut the tapestry off the frame I knotted sets of three warp ends together at the top, then trimmed the ends to 1cm (½in). At the bottom I formed tassels as shown on page 38.

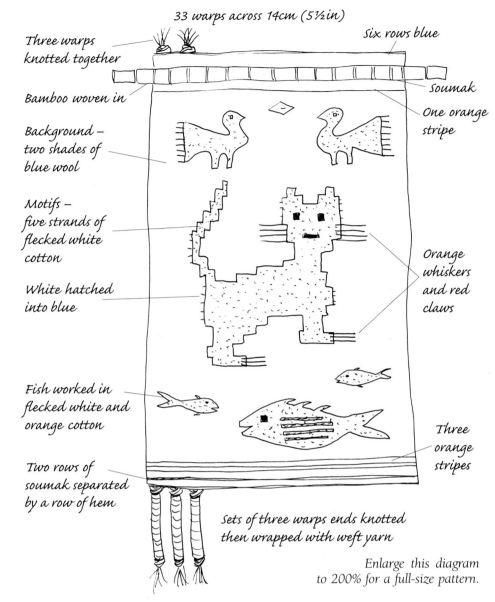

33 warps across 14cm (5½in)

Three warps knotted together

six rows blue

Bamboo woven in

Soumak

One orange stripe

Background – two shades of blue wool

Motifs – five strands of flecked white cotton

Orange whiskers and red claws

White hatched into blue

Fish worked in flecked white and orange cotton

Three orange stripes

Two rows of soumak separated by a row of hem

Sets of three warps ends knotted then wrapped with weft yarn

Enlarge this diagram to 200% for a full-size pattern.

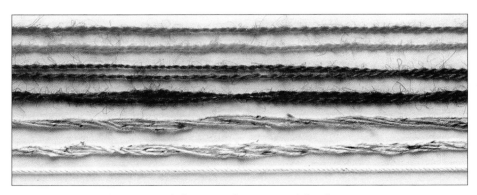

The cotton warp (bottom) and the six weft yarns used for this tapestry.

45

SIMPLE LANDSCAPE

Although the colour scheme of this tapestry is unreal, the design suggests a landscape with a boat on water and a setting sun. My initial sketch for this design was more realistic, but I decided to remove most of the detail to keep the weaving as simple as possible. It is now just a geometric type of pattern, but one that allows the imagination to make up the details, and turn it into a landscape.

I used a medium cotton yarn for the warp, and wound 46 warp threads spaced across 20cm (7¾in) of the frame. Again, I used wool rug yarn for the weft, in shades of red, orange, and yellow, and a dark purple.

Apart from the basic techniques described earlier, this project involves weaving a circle. Circles are really continuous curves, but to weave them so that they appear circular, and not oval, you must work the centre section with straight sides as shown in the step-by-step sequence opposite.

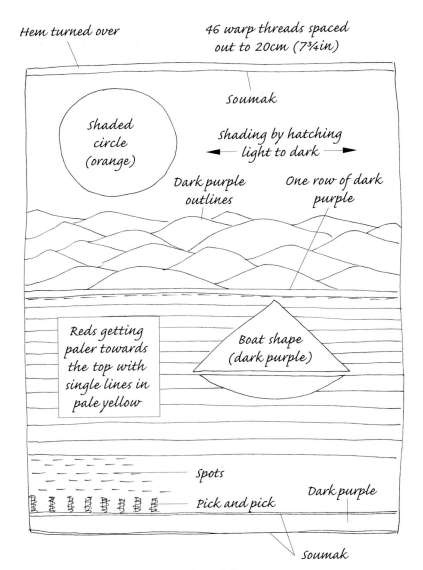

Hem turned over

46 warp threads spaced out to 20cm (7¾in)

Soumak

shaded circle (orange)

shading by hatching light to dark

Dark purple outlines

One row of dark purple

Reds getting paler towards the top with single lines in pale yellow

Boat shape (dark purple)

Spots

Pick and pick

Dark purple

Soumak

Enlarge this diagram to 150% for a full-size pattern.

The cotton warp yarn (bottom) and the shades of rug wool used for this tapestry.

If you want to work up your own design, try to keep it fairly simple. You do not have to be an artist, just scribble down your ideas. Remember that the drawing is not the end result, but a means of remembering something you found inspirational or interesting. By sketching it, you will tend to capture the essence of the subject.

You could take photographs, then use a small area of one, or a combination of several, as a starting point for a design. Collect cuttings or pictures, cut them up, and reassemble them in a different way to produce abstract designs.

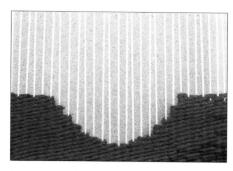

1. Weave the background on the left-hand side of the circle first, working up to just below the halfway point, shaping the curve by making taller and taller steps. Work the right-hand side by copying the stepping from the left.

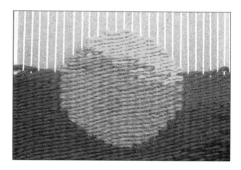

2. Fill in the bottom of the circle. When you get to the sides, weave them tall enough to make a true circle. Weave the background and the straight sides of the circle at the same time, weaving the colours into each other to join the slits.

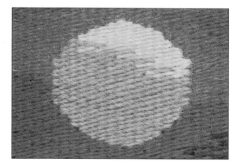

3. Weave the top of the circle, reversing the stepping from the lower half. Weave the background on each side of the top of the circle separately, remembering to continue hatching, then weave over the top of the sun shape, to complete the tapestry.

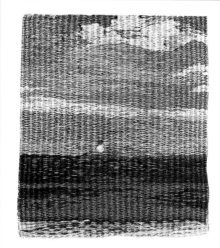

Seascape with lighthouse

In contrast to the landscape above, the texture of this tiny seascape, which was copied from a small watercolour sketch, is very fine. I used sewing silk and cotton for the weft, blending the colours to create a realistic looking sea and sky. It is reproduced full size.

COVER DESIGN

This tapestry (which was designed and woven specially for the book) illustrates different styles of weaving and a variety of techniques. It was woven on a fine cotton warp, using a mixture of fine wools and linen/cotton yarns for the weft. It measures 36 x 45cm (14 x 17¾in).

The centre panel with the tree, sun and moon was freely woven using distorted wefts, lozenge shapes, shading and hatching techniques. It is surrounded by borders of more formal patterns, where the slits have become part of the design. The bottom border imitates strips of interlocked weaving, and the bird and fish at the top are taken from the cat project on page 45. Hands often appear in my work, and the one in this piece symbolises the pleasures of working with our hands in a world that is becoming more and more mechanically minded.

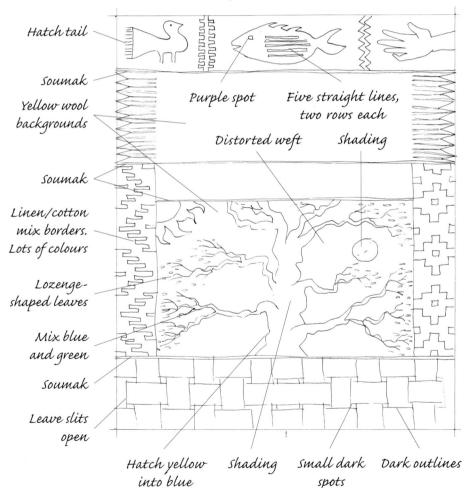

100 warp ends across 36cm (14in)

Hatch tail

Soumak

Yellow wool backgrounds

Soumak

Linen/cotton mix borders. Lots of colours

Lozenge-shaped leaves

Mix blue and green

Soumak

Leave slits open

Purple spot

Five straight lines, two rows each

Distorted weft · Shading

Hatch yellow into blue · Shading · Small dark spots · Dark outlines

Enlarge this diagram to 400% for a full-size pattern.

The fine cotton warp (bottom), and range of fine wools and linen/cotton yarns used for the weft of this tapestry.

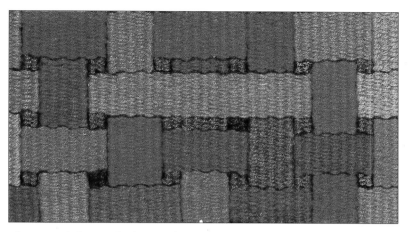

The vertical slits in the bottom border design are left open. The horizontal strips of weaving are outlined with a dark purple yarn so they appear to cross over and under each other.

This design imitates the experimental tapestry (right), where the strips of weaving actually do cross over and under each other creating a double layer of weaving.

The shaded effect of the moon was achieved by using a blend of pale yellows on the left, and hatching these into the darker greens on the right-hand side. Lots of blues, greens and purples, with touches of orange are shaded together to form the tree trunk. The background is hatched into the vertical edges of the tree trunk at regular intervals. The lozenge-shaped leaves have tiny yellow highlights created by mixing a fine yellow yarn into the red one, and allowing the yellow to show randomly.

Fish shapes are very easy to weave. This one is shaded in blues and greens with a purple eye and five red lines along the body. The pattern to the left of the fish is a traditional one, often found in Kelim rugs.

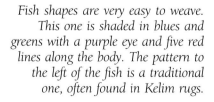

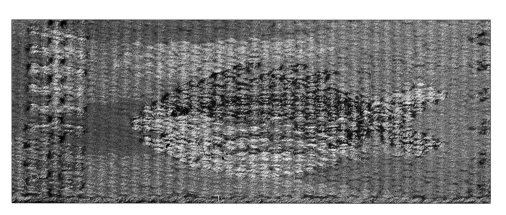

49

FURTHER TECHNIQUES

One of the things that makes tapestry weaving so exciting is the wide range of variations that are possible, and I have included some of these on the following pages. Up until now all the projects have been woven from the bottom up with the same thickness of weft yarns. Sometimes, however, a design works more easily if it is woven from the side, and you may want to have curved outer edges rather than straight ones. You can also vary the texture by using different thicknesses of weft and weaving fine yarns over single warp threads and thicker ones over two or more warp threads.

WARP AND WEFT VARIATIONS

When you have woven one or two of the early pieces, I suggest you try some different combinations of warp and weft. This way you will find out whether you prefer working with quite heavy materials on a large scale, or fine yarns for smaller, more detailed work. The relationship between the warp and weft, and the distance between the warp threads are both very important, and will influence the end result.

To illustrate this point, I wound three different warps on a frame then wove the same simple pattern on each warp.

I wound one warp with the same cotton yarn that I used for the sampler on page 14, spacing 12 warp threads across 7.5cm (3in) of the frame, leaving a relatively wide gap between them for a thick weft yarn to pass through. I then used a slightly finer yarn to wind 12 warp threads across 5cm (2in), to suit a finer weft. Finally I used an even finer yarn spacing the 12 warp threads across 3.5cm (1½in).

I used the same fine wool yarns all three tapestries. When winding the butterflies, however, I varied the number of threads in each set to match the different warps (see page 19).

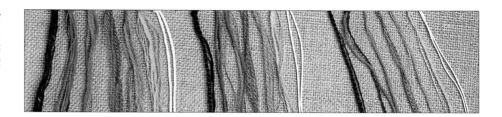

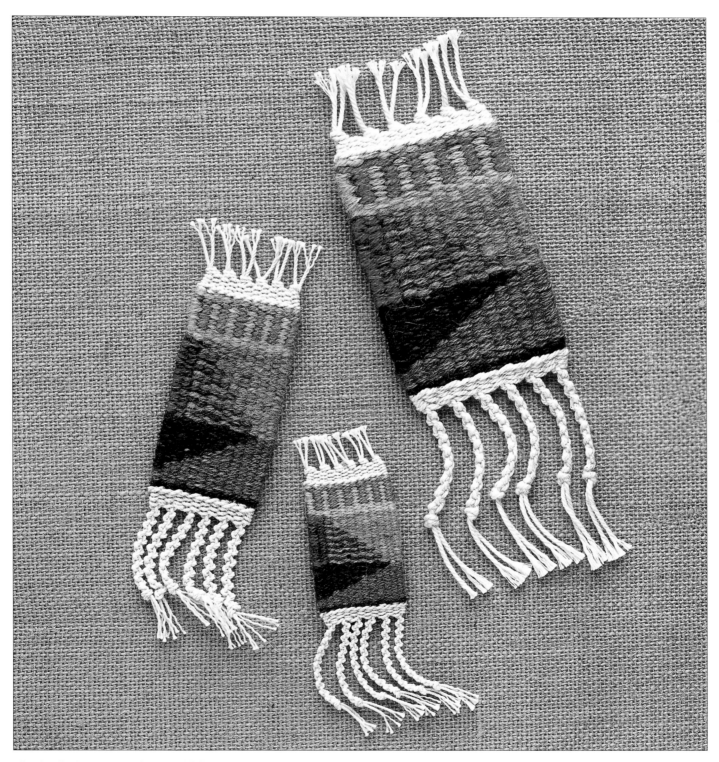

The finished tapestries show the difference in scale and texture that can be achieved by varying the warp and weft. Refer to page 38 for details on knotting the tassels.

Grey-toned labyrinth

This tapestry and the coloured one opposite were woven from the same pattern but with different warp and weft structures. They clearly show how you can create completely different images if you vary both the scale and the weft colours.

For this version, I spaced 56 medium-weight warp threads across 18cm (7in) of the frame. I used natural wools for the weft: a fine white wool for the tops of the walls, two shades of grey for their sides, a black for the ground, and a short length of red yarn for the figure.

I started the tapestry with a short hem, then, having enlarged the diagram to fit the width of the warp, I placed the pattern under the warp and outlined the design with a felt-tipped pen (see page 56).

To create more texture I wove most of the design over and under pairs of warp threads (this gives the same structure of twenty-eight warp threads as for the tapestry opposite). I changed to weaving under and over single warp threads for the tops of the walls and the small figure. This created a smooth texture to contrast with the roughness of the walls.

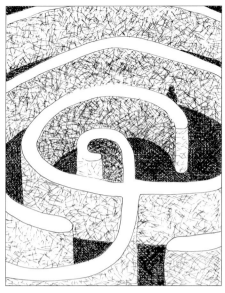

Enlarge this diagram to match the chosen width of your warp.

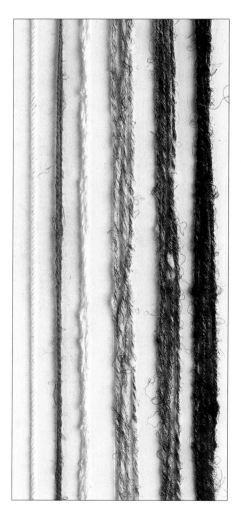

The warp yarn (left) together with the different widths of wool wefts used for the tapestry.

52

Coloured labyrinth

I used a very fine cotton for the warp of this tapestry, spacing 28 warp threads across 9cm (3½in) of the frame. I also used fine cotton yarns for the weft: a selection of reds, oranges and yellows for the walls, greens and blues for the ground, and short lengths of grey and black for the figure.

I wove a short hem before placing the enlarged diagram under the warp and transferring the outlines on to the warp threads.

I knotted a row of soumak, then worked up the design, weaving each block of colour separately, stitching up some of the slits and weaving the colours into each other at intervals elsewhere. I finished the top with a row of soumak and another short hem. Having cut the tapestry from the frame, I turned under both hems at the soumak and stitched them to the back of the tapestry (see page 66).

This tapestry and the grey-toned one opposite are reproduced at the same scale.

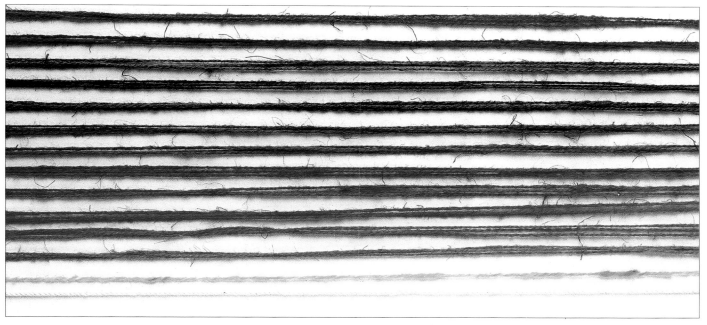

The cotton warp yarn (bottom) and the range of coloured cotton weft yarns used for the tapestry.

WEAVING FROM THE SIDE

All of the huge, intricately-woven, old tapestries in museums and stately homes across Europe were woven on their sides, with the warp running horizontally through the finished piece. One reason for working these large pieces in this way was that the weight of the weft was much greater than that of the warp, so, when finished, the tapestry would hang without distortion. In contrast, the modern tapestry in Coventry cathedral was woven on a vertical warp and, after a relatively short period, it already sags badly.

There are other good reasons for weaving a tapestry from the side, even for very small tapestries, where the weight is not important. Curves are easier to weave (and look much better) if they are horizontal on the warp. Fine lines are easier to weave across the warp, but almost impossible to weave going up it. You will quickly learn to see which way round a design works best.

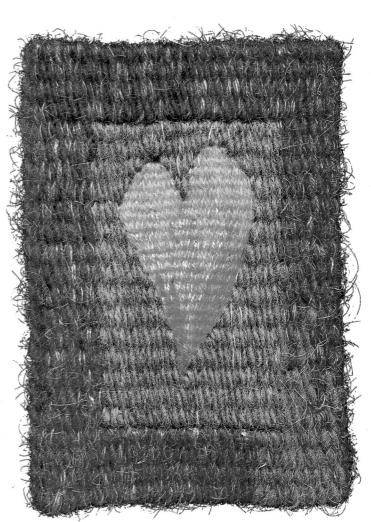

These two tapestries, both woven from the same design, are reproduced at the same scale. The left-hand one was woven from the bottom up, with 32 warps spaced across 10cm (4in) of the frame, whilst the other was woven from the side, with 46 warp threads spaced across 15cm (6in). Note how the bottom up version has ended up being rather squarer than the other.

Enlarge this diagram to match the size of the warp.

Heart

I used the diagram to weave the two tapestries opposite. The weaving method was exactly the same for both, but I worked the left-hand one from the bottom up and the other from the side.

Compare the heart shapes on each tapestry. Note how the one on the right, which was woven from the side, has smoother edges than the other, and it seems to fit more comfortably into the background.

The tapestries also show the difference in texture that can be achieved by varying the thickness of the weft. The green backgrounds and blue frames were worked with several strands of wool, woven over and under two warp threads at a time, to create a rough texture. The smoother heart shapes were worked with fine cotton yarns, woven over and under single warp threads.

I combined the top and bottom layers of warp threads as shown below for both tapestries – a good technique for getting lots of threads across a short warp. It saves you winding twice as many warp threads on the frame, but the warp ends are quite short when the tapestry is cut from the frame.

The weft yarns used for both the tapestries opposite. Note the difference in thickness between the blue and green woollen yarns, used for the background, and the orange, yellow and red cotton yarns used for the heart.

1. Wind the warp with the required number of warp threads, then weave a shed stick through both layers of threads, picking up one thread from the bottom layer between each top one.

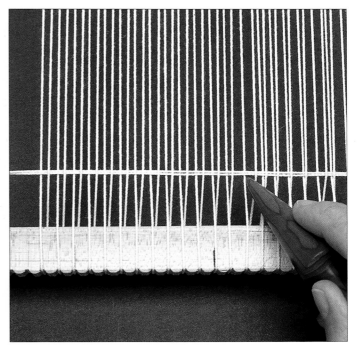

2. Referring to page 20, insert a double starter weft in the same shed as the stick (when the top and bottom warp layers are combined, both starter weft threads pass through the same shed). Push the shed stick up the warp, turn the frame and insert another double starter weft at the top. Use a bobbin to equalise the spaces between the warp threads.

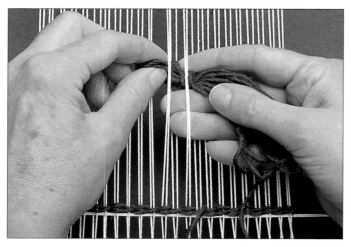

3. Work eight rows of hem, taking the weft thread over and under two warp threads at a time.

4. Knot a row of soumak over single warp threads. Place the pattern under the warp, aligning the design with the edge of the soumak, and then use a felt-tipped pen to mark the design on the warp threads.

5. Weave the design, working the border and background over and under pairs of warp threads, and the heart shape over and under single warp threads. Note the different textures achieved.

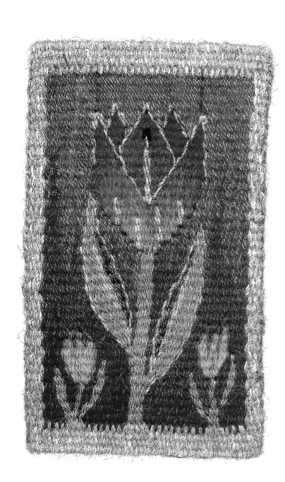

Tulip

The design of this tapestry is typical of those that are best woven from the side. The fine stalks and the outlines of the petals would be difficult to weave and would look very clumsy if they were woven from the bottom up. The warp consists of 45, medium-weight cotton threads spaced across 19cm (7½in) of the frame. The weft is a combination of wool and cotton yarns. After working a hem, I marked the outlines of the design on the warp with a felt-tipped pen (see opposite), then wove it using the basic techniques. When the work was cut from the frame, the hems were turned under and stitched to the back (see page 66).

The Parrot gets the last word

I like a sense of humour and often use a tongue-in-cheek title for my work. This parrot, which is part of a series of tapestries that have little women communicating with big birds, was woven from the side. The tapestry was mounted and framed in a similar manner to that described on pages 66–68. The tapestry measures 10 x 17cm (4 x 6¾in), and is mounted in a 17.5 x 24cm (7 x 9½in) frame.

CURVED AND IRREGULAR EDGES

Although the general aim of tapestry weaving is to have straight edges all round, some designs can look very effective with irregular sides or a curved or pointed top.

This type of finish works particularly well with small images that are woven from the side, but, sometimes, it can be equally effective on large pieces such as *Remember Marrakech* on page 90, where the centre arch continues beyond the top of the tapestry. In this case a hem was woven at the top, turned under and stitched to the back. However, when weaving a design with a curved edge from the side, you create the irregular shapes by weaving a waste filling before you start working on the design itself. This waste filling is very important – without it the tapestry would keep sliding down the warp and the shape would be lost.

Little owl

This design has straight sides and a curved top. It could be woven in the normal way, from the bottom upwards, but working it from the side makes it easier to create smooth curves – both those round the top and those that form the shape of the bird itself.

I decided to use 44 fine cotton warps spaced out to 13cm (5in) for this design. When creating the warp, I worked across the frame winding single warp threads in each of twenty notches. I then worked back to the start, winding a second thread in each notch. The other four threads were laid in randomly across the width of the warp, taking the thread diagonally across the back of the frame. I then used the starter weft to equalise the space between each warp thread.

The cotton warp yarn (bottom) and the range of weft yarns, including one with a fine gold thread, used for this tapestry.

Enlarge this diagram to 150% for a full-size pattern.

44 warp threads spaced over 13cm (5in)

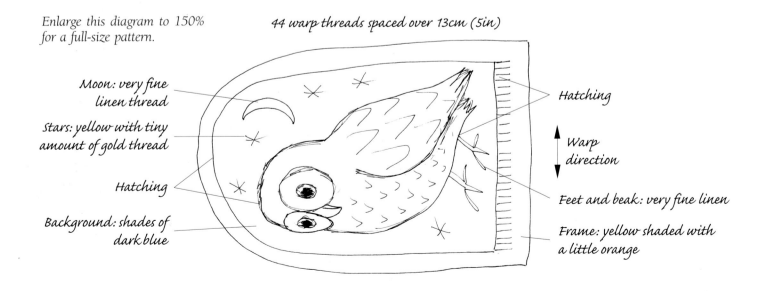

Moon: very fine linen thread

Stars: yellow with tiny amount of gold thread

Hatching

Background: shades of dark blue

Hatching

Warp direction

Feet and beak: very fine linen

Frame: yellow shaded with a little orange

I placed the pattern under the warp threads, positioning it to allow for the waste filling and hem, then used a felt-tipped pen to draw the curved outline and the basic shapes of the design on the warp threads. I then marked another curved line 1cm (½in) below to indicate the dividing line between the waste filling and the hem.

I used a length of the warp yarn to weave the waste filling below the lower curved line, working across the width of the warp and stepping back row by row to create the curved shape at the left-hand side. I then used a neutral coloured weft yarn to weave the hem, following the curve on the left-hand side.

Following the curve, I knotted a row of soumak from left to right, then started weaving the design. The top half of the tapestry was worked by following the curved outline of the design, ending with a row of soumak from left to right. To finish, I wove a hem right across the warp (there is no need to weave a waste filling). After cutting the tapestry from the frame, I carefully removed the waste filling. I turned the hems under, following the row of soumak on each side, then sewed them to the back of the tapestry.

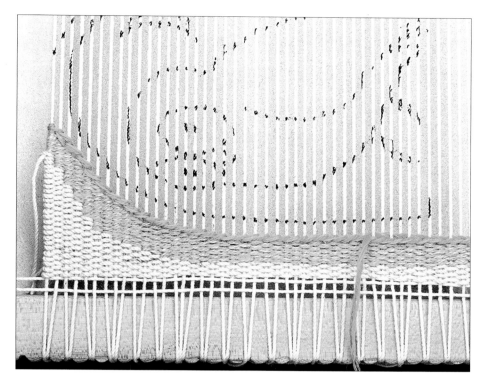

Little owl tapestry in progress. This photograph shows the hem, woven with warp yarn; the hem to be turned under and stitched to the back; and the row of soumak that forms the outer edge of the yellow/orange frame.

The finished tapestry. Notice that I used the hatching technique (see page 27) to join the right-hand yellow border (bottom of the design) to the blue background. A short length of hatching also joins the top of the curved border to the blue background.

All these small tapestries have curved and/or irregular edges and were woven from the side. A very fine cotton was used for the warp, and a mixture of linen and cotton embroidery thread for the weft. They were mounted on linen fabric and framed in simple box frames (see pages 66–68). Apart from *A Tortoise for Hanne* they are all reproduced at full size to show their detail and texture.

A Tortoise for Hanne

The sides of this tapestry, which measures 8.5 x 11cm (3¼ x 4½in), were kept straight except where the top of the tree curves out beyond the edge. The curve was achieved by tying four supplementary warp threads to the top and bottom of the frame alongside the left-hand edge, and using these to shape the top. When the piece was finished the extra warp ends were cut short and stitched to the back.

Treasures of the Nile

This is another example of how you can add interest to a design by shaping a tapestry. The technique is similar to the owl tapestry on page 58.

Forbidden fruit

In this piece I have purposely curved the edges slightly, by adding an extra thread on either side of the warp, and using these to widen the weaving in the middle.

Tiny owl on a starry night
Slightly distorted edges and a small amount of gold thread for the stars add interest to this owl tapestry.

Precious offering
Symbols from ancient Egyptian tomb paintings were the inspiration for this tapestry.

Wish you were here
A pointed top echoes the shape of the island in this tiny tapestry.

In principio
Simple lettering is not hard to weave and it can look very effective. It usually works best if it is woven from the side, and you may have to adapt the letters a little to avoid long thin lines in the warp direction.

CUSHIONS

From time to time I find it really satisfying to weave something that has a practical purpose, and cushion covers are an obvious choice for tapestry weaving. There are many subjects that would be suitable – you could weave simple, geometric designs, landscape and flower designs, or even, as I did with this selection birds or animals.

The back of each cushion is a piece of bought fabric, hand stitched to the tapestry all the way round, with a cushion pad inserted before the last side is sewn up.

One of the nice things about designing tapestries for cushions is that as they are not going to be hung on a wall, you do not have to be too serious about detail. You can have great fun just letting your mind wander. For example, the sleeping dog cushion, with all four of its legs stretched out in front and its head on an angle, does not look at all realistic, but it does fit into the cushion shape.

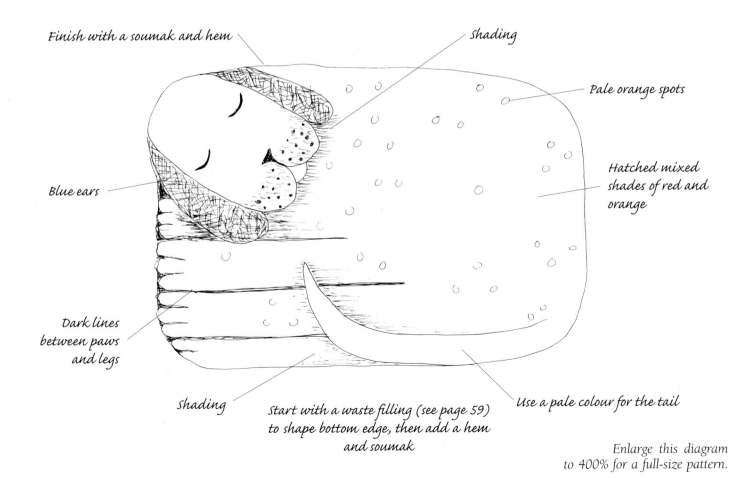

Finish with a soumak and hem

Shading

Pale orange spots

Blue ears

Hatched mixed shades of red and orange

Dark lines between paws and legs

Shading

Start with a waste filling (see page 59) to shape bottom edge, then add a hem and soumak

Use a pale colour for the tail

Enlarge this diagram to 400% for a full-size pattern.

62

Sleeping dog

This tapestry was woven on a linen warp spaced at 3 threads/cm (7 threads/in). Fine wool was used for the wefts.

The round corners at the bottom of both this design and that for the cat cushion overleaf were shaped by weaving a waste filling (see page 59), a 3cm (1¼in) hem and a row of soumak. I then used a felt-tipped pen to transfer the pattern on to the warp threads. I wove the design using the colours shown right, finishing with another row of soumak and a hem.

After cutting the weaving from the frame, I knotted pairs of warp ends together to secure them, folded under the hems along the row of soumak, then sewed on the backing fabric.

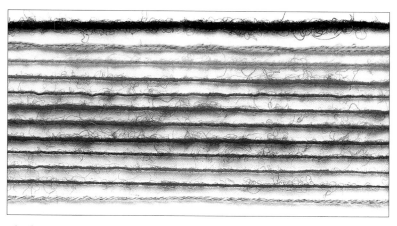

The linen warp yarn (bottom) and the range of fine wool wefts used for this tapestry.

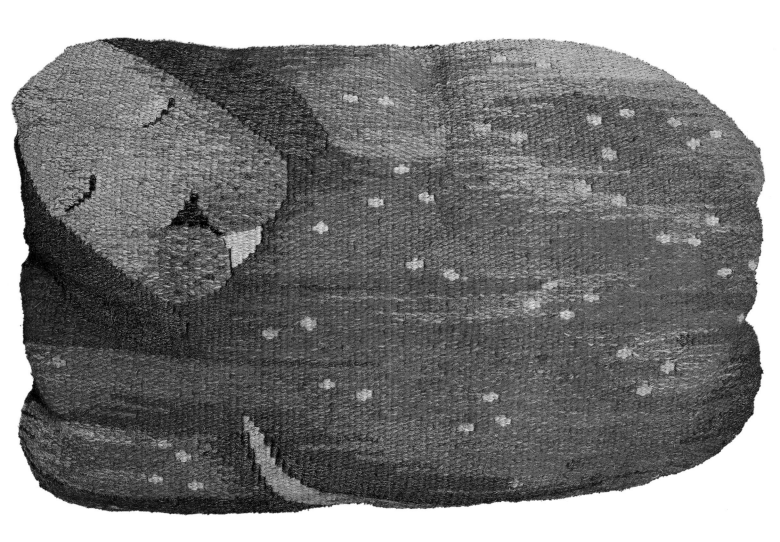

Sleeping cat

In contrast to the dog design on the previous page, which is full of curved lines and soft spots, this cat design has lots of straight lines and more pointed patterns and shapes.

The tapestry, which is roughly square in shape, was worked on a warp spaced at 3 threads/cm (7 threads/in). Eleven different colours of wool yarns were used for the weft.

Enlarge this diagram to 400% to make a full-size pattern.

Finish with a soumak and hem

Orange paws

Stitch up the vertical slits

Orange shaded with red

Mixed blue shades

Red diamonds and triangles

Start with a waste filling (see page 59) to shape bottom edge, then add a hem and soumak

64

Bird

This square cushion is woven on a warp spaced at 2 threads/cm (7 threads/in). Unlike the previous examples, this cushion has straight sides so it did not need a waste filling. I wove a 3cm (1¼in) wide hem and knotted a row of soumak. Having transferred the pattern on to the warp threads, I wove the design using a range of colours similar to that for the dog on page 63. I finished the weaving with a row of soumak and another hem, then made up the cushion in the usual way.

Enlarge this diagram to 400% to make a full-size pattern.

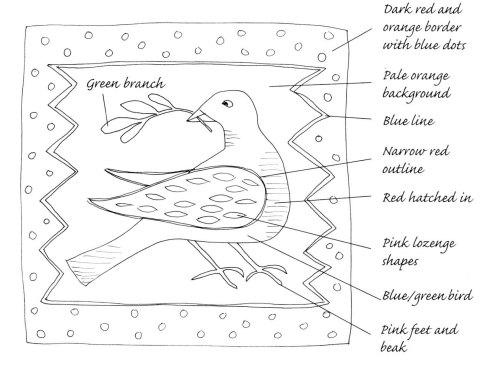

Green branch

Dark red and orange border with blue dots

Pale orange background

Blue line

Narrow red outline

Red hatched in

Pink lozenge shapes

Blue/green bird

Pink feet and beak

65

MOUNTING & FRAMING

Very small tapestries look a little lost on their own, and I think it is a shame to put them behind glass in ordinary picture frames. Instead, I stitch them on to a piece of plain linen fabric, stretch this over block-board, and make a simple box frame, painted to complement the colours of the weaving. Here, the tapestry measures 7.5 x 9cm (3 x 3½in), and the blockboard is 15cm (6in) square.

1. Cut the blockboard and the sides of the frame to size. I get my local timber supplier to do this, as I am not very accurate with a saw. Use acrylic paint to paint all sides of the frame pieces, and the back of the blockboard.

2. Cut an oversize piece of linen for the background. Use slip stitches to mark the centre square (the same size as the blockboard), then fold and crease the edges.

3. Cut the finished tapestry from the frame and trim off the excess warp ends.

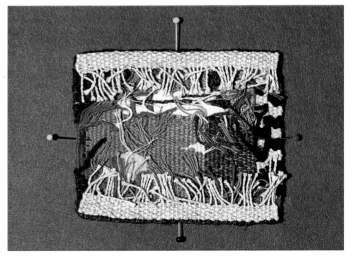

4. Fold the raw edges of the tapestry to the back, along the soumak, and gently iron the folds flat. Mark the centre of each side with a dressmaker's pin.

5. Slip stitch centre reference marks on the linen, centre the tapestry on these stitches, pin the tapestry to the linen, then use tiny invisible stitches to sew the tapestry to the linen.

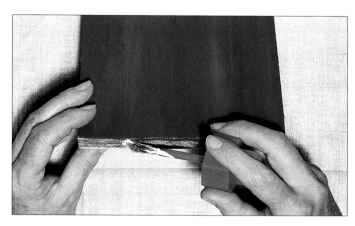

6. Place the linen, with the tapestry attached, face down on the work surface and position the blockboard on top. Lift one side of the blockboard and apply a layer of PVA glue to the edge.

7. Fold the linen up over the glued edge.

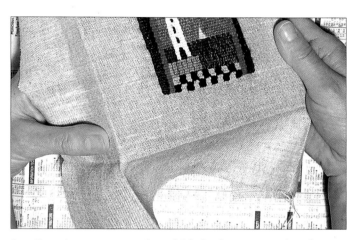

8. Glue the opposite edge, fold the linen over the glue, turn the whole piece over, then gently stretch the linen to centralise the tapestry on the blockboard.

9. When all four sides are glued, and you have checked that the tapestry is straight, cut the corners of the linen.

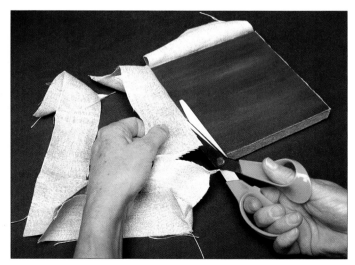

10. Using the sides of the blockboard as a guide, trim off all excess linen.

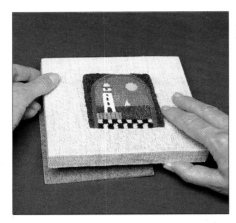

11. Place a hardboard spacer on the work surface, then place one corner of the blockboard, with the tapestry side up on top. The spacer creates a recess in the back of the frame

12. Nail the corners of two adjacent sides of the frame together.

13. Position the nailed sides round one corner of the blockboard, then nail the sides to the blockboard. Repeat steps 12–13 with the other two side to complete the frame.

The finished tapestry – mounted and framed. Add eye screws and string to the back of the blockboard and the tapestry can be hung on your wall.

Circus act

This tapestry is 19cm (7½in) square and is mounted in a 23.5cm (9¼in) square frame.

I wove the wide border by going over several warps, then under one warp in a random pattern. This produced a very textured surface to contrast with the finely woven central panel, and the brightly coloured diamond shapes.

I painted the background linen dark blue with watered-down acrylic paint, and left it to dry before sewing the tapestry on to it.

Messenger

The tapestry, shown full size below, is mounted in a ready-made frame constructed from rough, recycled wood, which I stained green to match the colours of the tapestry.

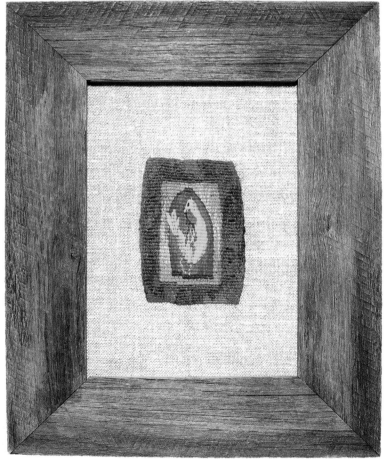

69

GALLERY

I enjoy working on a large scale, so I have included a few of my bigger tapestries. Although they were all woven on the loom shown on page 11, I used exactly the same techniques and methods of weaving as for tapestries woven on a frame.

Most of my tapestries tell a story and, sometimes, a series of tapestries will have the same theme such as a labyrinth.

SECRETS

Size: 49cm (19¼in) square

This colourful, finely-woven tapestry has a lively feel to it. It was woven on a fine wool warp, and the weft is a mixture of wool and very fine linen and cotton.

There is a lot of pattern detail in the dress, and the suggestion of a feather pattern in the parrot's wing. I have used distorted weft, with a lot of hatching to suggest folds in the dress. The hands were outlined using a darker yarn, and the fine vertical line between the centre and the border was woven around one warp thread, and randomly hatched into both to avoid slits. Round each star is a shading of paler blue that makes the stars look brighter.

Opposite
Detail taken from the centre panel of the tapestry.

GIVE ME SPACE

Size: 67 x 72cm (26½ x 28½in)

I have mixed many shades of similar colours in each area, hatching them into each other to blend them. The mask shows irregularly woven pick and pick vertical stripes on one cheek, and subtle shading in the eyes and nose. The line of the labyrinth has been softened by using a mix of yellow and turquoise to hatch it into the background on both sides.

At the top, the slits are left open in the checkerboard pattern, but between each row of squares, two rows of blue weft have been woven across the tapestry to hold it together.

This detail of the centre section of the tapestry shows how the turquoise labyrinth has been hatched into the yellow background to soften the edges of the labyrinth. The background, which is woven in different shades of yellow, has a herringbone structure created by weaving small blocks of colours across the width of the warp. Each block has diagonal sides (see page 28), and I changed the direction of the diagonals at regular intervals as I worked up the design.

THE SOUL NEEDS MORE SPACE THAN THE BODY

Size: 84 x 67cm (33 x 26½in)

Sometimes the inspiration for a tapestry comes directly from words I have heard or read. I start off by writing them down in my notebook, and sketching a few ideas, which gradually come together in a design. I usually work from a small colour sketch, with a full size pattern behind the warp.

This large tapestry was woven on my loom and is worked from the side. It is full of symbols and every space has been filled with patterns and subtle colour changes. It was woven on a fine, grey wool warp, using a mixture of wool, linen, and cotton yarns, for the weft.

This photograph shows the tapestry in progress on the loom. I wove it from the side because most of the shapes in the design, especially the long smooth lines of the woman' dress, worked best that way. The hem, which was turned under and stitched to the back when the tapestry was finished, is clearly visible at the bottom of the weaving.

In this photograph the tapestry is almost finished. The paper pattern, showing the right-hand snake border is clearly visible between the warp threads at the top.

AT THE STILL POINT

Size: 115 x 155cm (45 x 61in)

This large tapestry has a message of peace and a theme of spiritual rebirth. It has many symbols surrounding the centre of a labyrinth. All the plain background areas were woven over double warp threads, using weft butterflies made up of many strands of mixed yarns. For the detailed areas of the grapes and figure, I used single warp threads, and a much finer weft.

I wanted the vertical lines in the design to appear strong and definite, and the sky and birds to have a gently flowing horizontal feel to them, so I wove this tapestry from the bottom upwards. Although most of the shapes could have been woven from the side, the finished tapestry would have ended up looking rather different.

The two fish have finely woven tails and fins, and the subtle pattern on their backs is woven using the pick and pick technique with shades of blue and green.

These two photographs were taken while the tapestry was on the loom. Although the different parts of the weaving are all at different levels, I try to keep them as even as possible. Note that all the butterflies currently in use have been stuck into the top of the warp.

This detail of the bottom centre panel shows quite clearly the difference in texture between the background area and that of the birds and figure. I used multiple strands of mixed yarns for the background wefts, weaving them over and under two warp threads. The birds and the figure are worked with finer wefts, woven under and over single warp threads.

The pattern used for the labyrinth in the centre of this tapestry is a mirror image of that shown on page 52. Labyrinths have fascinated me for a very long time, and they occur in many of my tapestries, usually as a flat pattern rather than as a three-dimensional image. I like the mystery they suggest, and I actually built a large one in my garden while weaving the same pattern in the tapestry.

JOURNEY

Size: 116 x 134cm (46 x 52½in)

'The future enters into us, in order to transform itself in us, long before it happens'. These words, by the Austrian writer Rainer Marie Rilke, were the starting point for the tapestry. It includes various signs and symbols that signify our journey through life.

This detail shows some of the symbols that often appear in my tapestries.

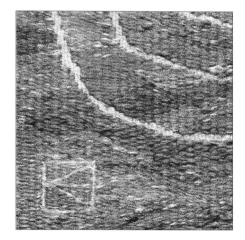

The bottom left-hand corner of the labyrinth and my signature which I weave into all my large tapestries.

The top right-hand corner of the tapestry, showing clearly the difference in texture between the thicker background, woven over double warps, and the finer weaving in the people, and the line of the labyrinth.

ALL SHALL BE WELL

Size: 98 x 99cm (38½ x 39in)

This tapestry consists of three separate panels, which hang together as a group, as shown below. They were woven from the side on a grey, fine wool warp, and a range of fine wool, linen, and cotton yarns was used for the weft.

I particularly enjoyed mixing and blending the colours to weave the blue starry dress, and the green robe with the sun on it.

To ensure that they would hang straight, I mounted each panel on a board, which was cut to the exact size and covered in blue linen fabric. When the weaving was cut from the loom, I turned the hems to the back, then sewed the tapestry to the linen.

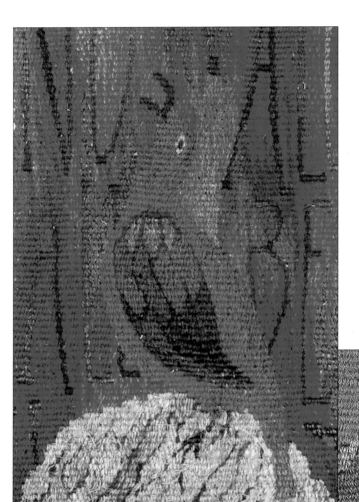

This detail from the left-hand panel of All Shall Be Well shows the bird on the woman's head. The bird itself is quite plain, but the wing has a detailed pattern of stylised feathers, where each shape is outlined in dark blue. The woman's hair was woven with very fine orange and brown wool, and thick, rough linen yarn, which made the grey wool warp show slightly in places.

The background is woven with many shades of blue, hatched and blended into each other. The lettering is only partly visible behind the two figures in the two side panels and, because the tapestry was woven on its side, I decided to make the lettering tall and thin, with very short horizontal lines.

This detail of a pomegranate in the woman's hand and some of the folds of her dress, shows distorted weft, and outlining. I used a mix of vibrant pale blue yarns for the dress, to make the figure stand out from the dark background. The weft for the stars was natural wool mixed with some fine pale blue yarn to make them appear to be part of the dress fabric.

This detail of the top part of the centre panel shows hatching below the windows and shading in the blue background. Although I have blended many different shades of colour in all parts of the tapestry, I have used the same colours in all three panels. I wanted to avoid using straight lines, both horizontal ones across the warp and vertical ones along the warp threads, so, in the area below the windows and where the grey frame is hatched into the blue, I stepped the vertical slits.

The green man from the right-hand panel sprouts leaves from his face and head. It was exciting, and quite a challenge, to weave him. I used the same rough linen yarn as that for the woman's hair opposite, but, this time, I mixed it with fine wool in shades of green and blue. The sun on the man's green garment is similar to the one on the centre panel.

MOROCCAN COURTYARD

Size: 50 x 85cm (19½ x 33½in)

In this decorative tapestry the symmetrical, and ordered design reflects the stillness and tranquillity of a secluded courtyard. It was woven on a fine wool warp, using a range of vegetable dyed wool yarns for the weft.

The border at the bottom starts with simple squares, then there is an area of interlocked strips of weaving, similar to those for the cover design for the book (see page 48). At the sides, the red weft stripes continue beyond the edges of the tapestry, and are then wrapped.

After the tapestry was finished the hem was turned under at the top and bottom, and thick wool-wrapped cords were sewn along these edges. In the bottom left-hand corner a bunch of wrapped threads and plaits finish the decoration.

NO LIMITS

Size: 160 x 185cm (63 x 72¾in)

Hot air balloons floating away over the rooftops, with the gulls looking on. The balloons are woven on single warp threads, using fine embroidery wool, and as a contrast the sky is woven on double warps, using different shades of natural, handspun linen.

SACRED LAKE

Size: 60 x 135cm (23½ x 53in)

I find travelling and visiting other cultures a great source of inspiration, and always come back with sketches and photographs, some of which eventually appear in my work. Sometimes there is no obvious connection because I have re-worked the images so many times there is hardly anything left of the original. But at other times, as in this weaving the images still very clearly reflect the culture they came from.

In Sacred Lake I have used images from ancient Egyptian tomb paintings, putting them together into a design, which was woven from the side. The background is a mixture of handspun flax, wool, and some real camel hair.

This detail of the bottom left-hand corner of the tapestry shows a hand holding the key of life – the ankh.

I wanted to suggest a white, diaphanous fabric for the sleeve, so I mixed a small amount of white cotton with the wool used for the hand. When weaving the sleeve I worked the weft under and over two warps to create a rougher texture to contrast that of the hand.

This detail shows the sacred lake with plants growing around it and a serpent's head. I wove the chevron pattern of the water with mixtures of pale and dark blues. I alternated the weaving of the diagonals from one side of the warp to the other (see page 28). This tapestry was woven on its side – compare these chevron shapes with those on Give me space on page 72 which was woven from the bottom up. Most of the tapestry was worked over and under two warp threads, but, for smaller areas, such as the serpent's eye and the plants around the lake, I worked over and under single warp threads to create a finer texture and to include more detail.

Two groups of papyrus separated by the thicker, ridged stem of the palm which was woven using the pick and pick technique . To contrast the thick textured background, I wove the papyrus flowers and buds over and under one warp thread with very fine wool wefts. At the top, I left slits and allowed them to open up slightly. I stylised the shape of the plants and other images in this tapestry in much the same way as the ancient Egyptians did on their tomb paintings.

ANNA'S WINDOW

Size: 85 x 140cm (33½ x 55in)

When I started designing this tapestry, I knew that I needed to weave the view out of the window from the side, so that all the tree trunks would fit in and look good . But I also wanted the rug and the checked floor effect at the bottom to have a strong horizontal look. So in the end I decided to compromise. I started off with a fine warp, weaving the two window panels from the side, using natural brown wool for the tree trunks, with white, roughly spun silk for the sky, and ground. I then wove the surround from the bottom up on a thicker warp, using mostly handspun flax for the weft, with some coloured wool for the window frame and rug. I left the warp threads unwoven in the window panels, and when all the pieces were ready, I slipped the view into position on top of the bare warp threads, and stitched everything together.

Detail showing the view into the woods.

SOLITUDE

Size: 100cm (39in) square

I love sitting quietly on a rock looking out to sea. In this tapestry, I wove the outer border areas with mixtures of very thick, natural coloured wool, adding more texture by weaving the weft over two or more warps at random. To suggest the surfaces of the rocks, I used very fine wool to weave some thin green and turquoise lines through the textured areas. The rest of the tapestry was woven over and under two warps, except for the small figure which was woven over and under one. I used yellow wool mixed with a strand of white to make the sun look hazy in the pale blue sky.

REMEMBER MARRAKECH?

Size: 90 x 140cm (35 x 55in)

A mixture of symbols and formal patterns make up this colourful image. It was woven on a linen warp, and for the weft I used handspun, natural linen together with wool which I dyed with acid dyes. I find the unevenness of hand dyed yarns much more attractive than the perfection of commercially dyed ones. The centre arch continues beyond the top edge of the tapestry, and I have used rows of soumak knotting to define the different areas.

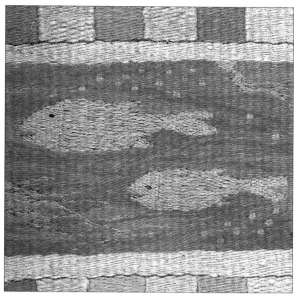

The top of the palm tree in the centre. I used five or six strands of weft yarn together in the blue background, and to shade it, I gradually mixed in darker and darker blues while leaving out the lighter ones.

Two fishes and some weed from the pond.

Below

Part of the border at the bottom of the tapestry. To make the triangles tall enough, the diagonal sides are shaped by high steps (see pages 28–29).

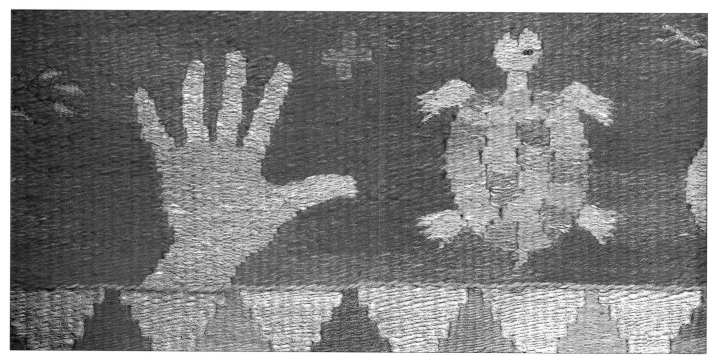

FRAGMENTS OF A FRIENDSHIP

Size: 148 x 152cm (58 x 60in)

This tapestry is a collage of different images, put together as a reminder of an important friendship. The vine and grapes look quite realistic and continue into a more formal pattern on the orange frame around the masks. I spent a long time making the books look real, suggesting their titles rather than trying to weave the actual words. My son, who is a keen sailor, corrected the angles of the boats on my drawings many times before allowing me to weave them.

ONE FOR EVERY OCCASION

Size: 140 x 145cm (55 x 57in)

This tapestry is part of a series of slightly surreal work. The woman in front of the mirror has removed her 'real' face and is waiting to put on another one. The masks were woven with wool on a background of rough handspun linen weft. Behind the framed masks, the background imitates a simplified Indian shawl pattern. It has wide borders of pick and pick, and a pattern of lozenge shapes in the centre. I mixed different amounts of purple wool with the background linen to weave the flowing purple hair, and used the distorted weft and hatching techniques to make it look lively.

FREE AS A BIRD

Size: 150cm (59in) square

This tapestry has a dreamlike theme – in fairy tales everything is possible. Women turn into birds and fly out into the night sky. The dovecotes in the centre are quite angular and definite, and contrast well with the lively feel of the surrounding sky which was achieved using the distorted weft technique and lots of shading and hatching.

BODY LANGUAGE

Size: 120cm (47¼in) square

The inspiration for this tapestry came when I walked to the top of a hill on a very windy day: I felt as if I could just take off and fly around. In this tapestry, the border is so wide and colourful that it has become more important than the central image. I really enjoyed weaving the wild shapes of the women flying through the trees. I distorted the weft so much, weaving the branches at acute angles, that it became quite hard to make the finished tapestry hang straight. In contrast, the small centre panel is very calm and simple.

INDEX

bamboo 12, 15, 36–37, 38, 42, 44
basic techniques 14–37
birds 42–43, 44, 48, 49, 57, 58–59, 65, 76, 77, 82, 94
boats 46, 92
borders 48, 56, 59, 65, 69, 70, 75, 84, 89, 91, 93, 95

cats 44–45, 48, 64
circles 28, 46–47,
curved edges 34, 50, 54, 58–61
curves 28–29 *see also circles*
cushions 62–65

diagonal shapes 14, 15, 28–29, 73, 87, 91
distorted weft 14, 15, 32–33, 42, 48, 70, 82, 93, 94, 95

felt-tipped pen 12, 52, 56, 57, 59
figures 52, 53, 76, 77, 82, 89
fish 44–45, 48, 49, 76, 91
flowers 57, 87
frames, picture 57, 60, 69
frames, weaving 8, 10–11, 16–17, 36, 37, 50, 70
framing 13, 66–69

grapes 76, 92

hair 82, 93
hands 48, 87
hatching 14, 15, 27, 31, 42, 44, 47, 48, 49, 58, 59, 62, 65, 70, 72, 73, 82, 83, 93, 94
heart 54–56
hem 14, 15, 20–21, 22, 38, 39, 40, 46, 52, 53, 56, 57, 58, 59, 62, 63, 64, 65, 75, 80, 84
horizontal stripes 14, 15, 24–25 *see also straight lines*

irregular edges 58–61

labyrinths 52–53, 70, 72–73, 76–77, 79
landscape 46–47
lettering 61, 82
loom 8, 10–11, 70, 74–75, 76

masks 72, 92, 93
materials 8–13
mounting 13, 60, 66–69, 80

outlining 14, 15, 34–35, 46, 48, 49, 65, 70, 82

pick and pick 14, 15, 26, 40, 42, 46, 72, 76, 87, 93

seascape 47
shading 14, 15, 31, 40, 46, 48, 49, 62, 64, 70, 72, 94
shed stick, 12, 20, 36, 55
sky 47, 76, 85, 88, 89, 94

slits, vertical 14, 15, 30, 39, 40, 42, 48, 49, 53, 64, 70, 72, 83, 87
soumak 14, 15, 22–23, 25, 26, 27, 29, 30, 31, 33, 35, 39, 40, 42, 44, 46, 48, 53, 56, 59, 62, 64, 65, 66, 90
spots 14, 15, 24–25, 46, 48,
straight lines 15, 21, 32, 42, 48, 64, 83
sun 40–41, 46, 48, 80, 83, 89

tassels 14, 15, 37, 38–39, 42, 44, 51
texture 32, 50, 51, 52, 56, 57, 60, 69, 77, 79, 87, 89
trees 48, 60, 88, 91, 95

vertical slits *see slits, vertical*
vertical stripes *see pick and pick*

warp and weft variations 50–51
warp ends
   cutting 14, 15, 36–37
   knotting 15, 37, 38–39, 42, 44, 63
   wrapping 38, 40, 44
warps, winding 16–17, 40, 42, 44, 46, 52, 53, 54, 55, 57, 58
warp yarns 8
   cotton 15, 16, 42, 44, 46, 48, 53, 57, 58, 60
   linen 40, 63, 90
   wool 70, 74, 80, 82, 84

weaving from the side 50, 54–57, 58, 61, 74, 80, 82, 87
weft butterflies 18–19
weft, starter 20–21, 36, 37, 55, 58
weft, waste filling 58–59, 62, 63, 64
weft yarns 8
   camel hair 86
   cotton 40, 44, 47, 53, 55, 57, 60, 70, 74, 80, 87
   embroidery wool 85
   gold thread 58, 60
   flax 63, 86, 88
   joining 24
   linen 42, 58, 60, 70, 74, 80, 82, 83, 85, 90, 93
   linen/cotton mixture 48
   metallic threads 40
   preparing 18–19
   silk 47, 88
   wool 15, 40, 42, 44, 46, 51, 52, 55, 57, 63, 64, 70, 74, 80, 82, 84, 86, 87, 88, 89, 90, 93

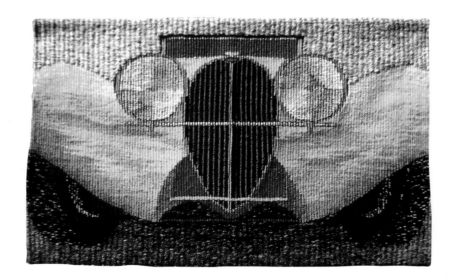

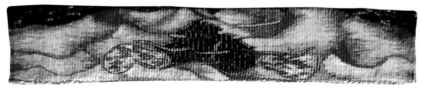

BUGATTI

A tongue in cheek image of a beautiful car admiring its own reflection in a puddle on the ground.